Ancient Egypt before Writing

From Counting to Hieroglyphs

by
Alicia Meza

DORRANCE PUBLISHING CO., INC.
PITTSBURGH, PENNSYLVANIA 15222

All Rights Reserved
Copyright © 2001 by Alicia Meza
No part of this book may be reproduced or transmitted
in any form or by any means, electronic or mechanical,
including photocopying, recording, or by any information
storage and retrieval system without permission in
writing from the publisher.

ISBN # 0-8059-4970-4
Printed in the United States of America

First Printing

For information or to order additional books, please write:
Dorrance Publishing Co., Inc.
643 Smithfield Street
Pittsburgh, Pennsylvania 15222
U.S.A.
1-800-788-7654

Or visit our website and online catalogue at *www.dorrancepublishing.com*

To Egypt, the beloved land
Gregory Johnson
Faiza Haikal

For Maria Ellul

Contents

Preface vii
Acknowledgments ix
List of Illustrations xi
List of Abbreviations xiii
Abstract xiv

Chapter One
Introduction 1
    Goals of the Study

Chapter Two
Regional Description and Historical Information 7
    Background about 4000 B.C. Mesopotamia and Egypt.

Chapter Three
Discussion of Tokens' Role in Mesopotamia .17
    Influence in Economy and Social Development.

Chapter Four
Discussion of Tokens and Graffiti Pot-Marks 22
    Egyptian and Mesopotamian Proto-signs.

Chapter Five
Discussion of the Archaeological Evidence .30
    Hoffman, Fairsevis, Bard, Harlan, and Johnson.

Chapter Six
Regional Archaeological Analysis 40
    Predynastic Egypt, the Susiana Plains, and Warka.

Chapter Seven
Archaeological Reports and Publications 49

Conclusions 63
Appendix 68
Endnotes 80
Bibliography 85

Preface

The invention of writing evolved in Mesopotamia during the last part of the fourth millennium B.C. The development of a counting token system into a more abstract system of writing was proposed by Denise Schmandt-Besserat. Its possible distribution from Mesopotamia into the Nile Valley region suscitated my interest. Since at this time period many socio-economic changes were occurring in both regions, I decided to study their relationship.

As much as the intellectual innovation of writing influenced the development of Mesopotamian social stratification, I decided to investigate the development of writing and social stratification in Predynastic Egypt. A parallel Egyptian social development to the Mesopotamian social structure may have been possible by exchange of information and interaction involving both regions. Perhaps they engaged in the exchange of goods and raw materials using a counting device to facilitate trade. If Egyptian Predynastic towns were dealing with each other, they probably participated in an interregional system of which Mesopotamia also was a partner.

Mesopotamian influence on the development of Egyptian culture and writing has long been debated in Egyptology since the early days of Petrie and Caton-Thompson. Nevertheless, Mesopotamian influence on Egyptian Predynastic art and architecture, and the later Egyptian adoption of the Mesopotamian seal have been accepted. Although these adaptations always acquired a distinctive, indigenous Egyptian style, Mesopotamian influence is embedded in Egyptian cultural development.

The purpose of this study is then to investigate the possibility of the existence of a counting system in Egypt that may have developed into a writing system; the consequences that this development may have had in the development of a pristine state formation in Predynastic Egypt; and when and how this development may have begun. Was it a gradual, heterogeneous occurrence throughout the Nile Valley or was it a unique isolated event as always believed? How integrated those Predynastic villages or towns were with each other and what relationship, if any, they had with an outside system, such as Mesopotamia?

Acknowledgments

I want to express my deepest thanks, first to my sponsor, Professor Gregory Johnson, without his unending support and encouragement this work would never have succeeded. To Professors Edward Bendix, Francis P. Conant, Daniel Bates, and Thomas McGovern for giving me knowledge. My thanks also to Professor Faiza Haikal for her confidence to accomplish my work.

I also must thank Mary Gow and Diane Bergman at the Wilbour Library at the Brooklyn Museum for those lengthy hours of research and assistance. To Dr. James Allen from the Metropolitan Museum of Art for his valuable indications and help.

To Drs. Thomas von der Way, Gunther Dreyer and Manfred Bietak who also assisted me with their valuable indications. And, finally, I also must thank all my professors at Queens College who silently and patiently guided me into the world of Anthropology.

Any problems of interpretation of all the data here included as well as the conclusions are, however, solely mine.

List of Illustrations

Figure

The Narmer and Libyan Palettes. 4

The Qustul Incense Burners. 5

Matmar Tags and Perforated Objects. 15

Gaming Pieces from Saqqara. 26

Painted "Niwt" Sign from Abadiyeh. 32

Bullae and Tokens from Mesopotamia. 35

Wavy Lines, "Niwt" Sign and "Z" Sign. 50

The Scorpion Palette. 52

The Sacred Marriage. 56

The Sayala Seals. 61

Appendix. 68

List of Abbreviations

Am. Anthro.	American Anthropologist
ASAE	Annales du Service des Antiquites de l'Egypte
BSAE	British School of Archaeology in Egypt
BULL. INST. D'EG.	Bulletin de l'Institut d'Egypte
BULL. SOC. GEOG. D'EG.	Bulletin de l'Institut d'Egypte
CHRON. D'EG.	Chronique d'Egypte
EEF	Egypt Exploration Fund
EES	Egypt Exploration Society
JAA	Journal of Anthropological Archaeology
JARCE	Journal of the American Research Center in Egypt
JEA	Journal of Egyptian Archaeology
JFA	Journal of Field Archeology
MDAIK	Mitteilungen des Deutschen Institut fur Agyptische Altertumskunde in Kairo
ZAZ	Zeitschrift fur Agyptische Sprache und Altertumskunde

Abstract

An investigation is conducted here to elucidate a possible use of a counting device system in Egypt similar to the one developed during the fourth millennium B.C. in Mesopotamia. This token system may have been an essential step in the development of the first writing system in the ancient world. Moreover, Mesopotamia also was, at this time, developing its first state formation within the Warka and Susa areas. A model proposed by Schmandt-Besserat indicates how influential the innovation of counting and the subsequent writing system were to the development of Mesopotamian social stratification.

Gregory Johnston's archaeological analysis of the area corroborates a very early state formation at the beginning of the Middle Uruk Period, about the same time when the transition from counting to cuneiform may have occurred.

If the development of Ancient Egyptian writing was in part based on the same type of transition, from counting to hieroglyphs, using a Mesopotamian idea for such innovation but adapted to an Egyptian system, perhaps there are traces of such devices in the archaeological record.

A correlation is made here of proto-signs from both areas, Mesopotamia and Egypt. A review of the archaeological record employing Johnson's statistical method used for Mesopotamia's archaeological analysis also is done to find a possible early social stratification being developed in Egypt more or less at the same time period than in Sumer and in Elam. The results corroborate that Egyptian Predynastic towns during the fourth millennium B.C. were being integrated into a regional system that was probably connected with an outside region. The questions proposed here are an open road for further research.

Chapter One

Introduction

During the fourth millenium B.C. the Mesopotamian region experienced unprecedented cultural and social changes that led to the invention of writing and to the first state formations in the area. For instance, the counting system that had been used since the eighth millennium B.C. changed from a concrete device of employing counters or tokens, to identify a single item, to a new abstract system[1] that used diverse forms of complex tokens for reckoning things. Complex tokens contained markings to convey more information. Therefore, the innovation in the reckoning system rapidly paved the way for the development of writing. This social and intellectual development was also adopted in southwestern Asia and probably in the Nile Valley area.

The development of reckoning things into a writing system may have had significant consequences for Mesopotamian political and economic life. For instance, a rapid increase in trade and competition for resources and goods may have led to the creation of the monopoly of production and distribution centers for goods. This may have then resulted in the development of leaderships, social stratification, and subsequently, state formation (Johnson, 1977: 481-94).

Regional archaeological analysis provide us with a method to calculate the time period when Warka in southern Mesopotamia and Susa in southwestern Iran developed their first state systems in those areas. The studies of both Denise Schmandt-Besserat and Gregory Johnson coincide in their predictions of the time periods when these intellectual and sociopolitical changes occurred. By using their theoretical models, an appraisal of previous research done by Egyptologists within Predynastic Egypt is attempted here.

During the fourth millenium B.C. significant changes also transformed the Nile Valley area. The idea of Egyptian people living in isolation and

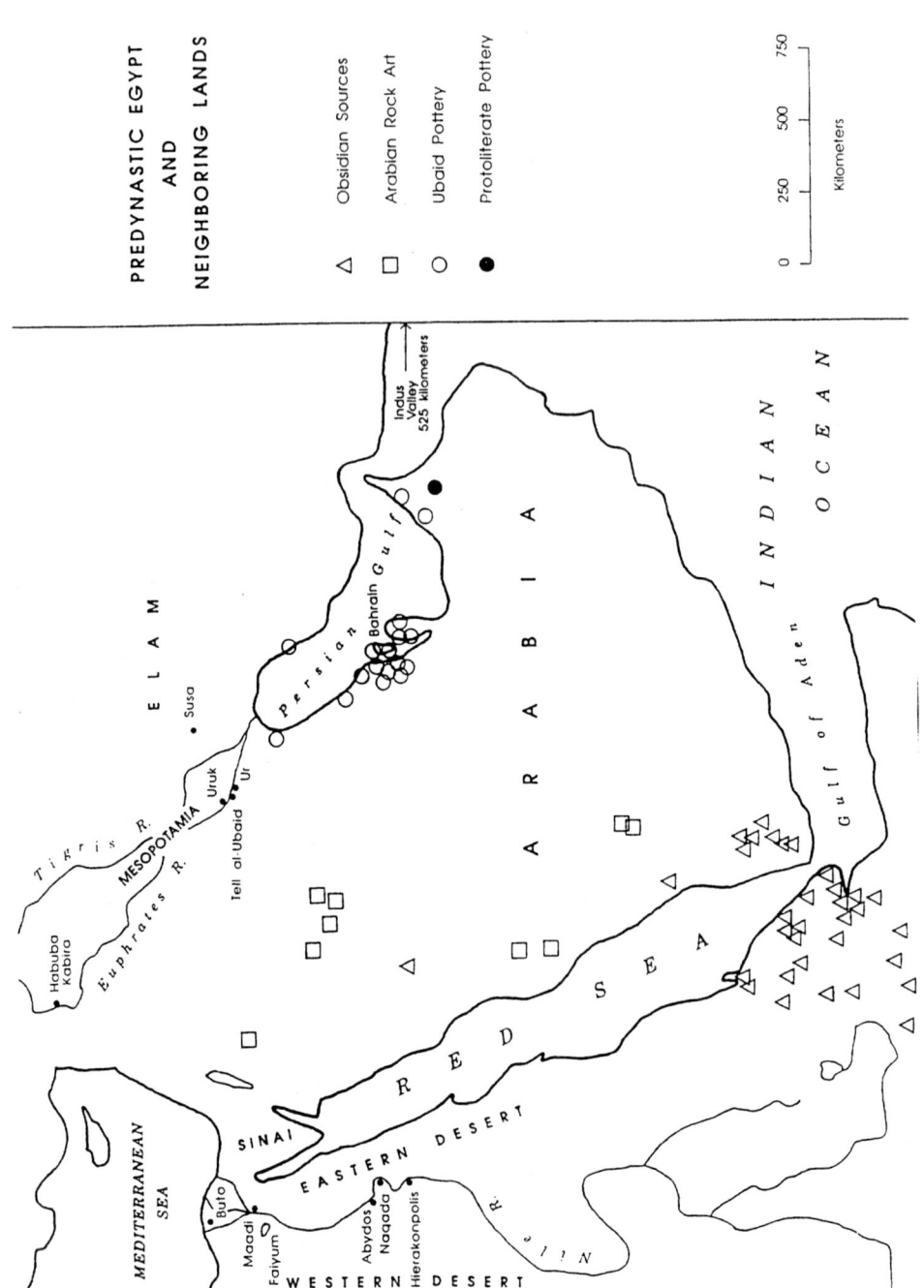

developing their own self-contained culture, as it has been assumed during the early years of Egyptology, is an idea that originated in Malinowski's own experiences. This idea will be challenged here, following Barth's innovation that people always live in interaction with other people. A notion of cultures in contact as a necessary basis for social development also has been proposed by Susan Lees. There are no closed systems, and boundaries can always be culturally crossed as has been asserted by Rapaport (Conant, 1993: class notes).

Following up on the ideas expressed above this paper will try to demonstrate that Egypt had parallel social and intellectual developments to those of Mesopotamia and southwestern Iran during the fourth millennium B.C. The studies done by Hoffman, Fairsevis, Harlan, and Bard on Egyptian Prehistory are used as evidence and support for this thesis. Their archaeological work and their own assertions that Egypt was a stratified society well before the beginning of the third millennium B.C. also will serve as part of the evidence used here.

The precise idea I have followed is that Egypt never generated its pristine state formation in isolation, but that Mesopotamia was an important element in Egyptian social development. Moreover, pristine state formation in Egypt never occurred in the idealistic way of a sole state reuniting the whole country and emerging, as the primeval mound, out of the waters of the chaos. This is a very tempting ancient Egyptian cosmological idea, but nevertheless nonpragmatic because for an area so diverse and large as Egypt it is geographically impossible to achieve a sole state formation in a pristine stage. Systems emerging in a dotted layout in a gradually heterogenous way is a more probable possibility. This notion can be inferred from the diversity of towns and centers that proliferated during the Predynastic Period throughout the country and that later were the basis for the formation of the Lower and Upper Egypt kingdoms from the historical tradition.

Social interaction and trade among those cities had to be tenuous at the beginning. But with a new improvement in the reckoning system, local exchange may have improved, extending to other outside regions such as the Mediterranean, Palestine, and Mesopotamia. Furthermore, Egypt was able to trade and interact with the rest of Africa throughout contacts with Nubia and Libya, as it is attested in rock drawings and later in tomb wall-paintings.

Cultural interaction may have also meant conflict; there is no doubt about it. Symbolically, there are depictions of early Predynastic conflicts among fortified cities, such as those represented in the Libyan palette, and the incense burners from Qustul (fig. 1,2). Perhaps competition for trade routes, markets, and access to natural resources also was a reason for conflict and for trying to improve commercial communications. That the outcome from these events acquired unexpected dimensions also is not an alien possibility. In human

The Narmer Palette

Reverse

Obverse

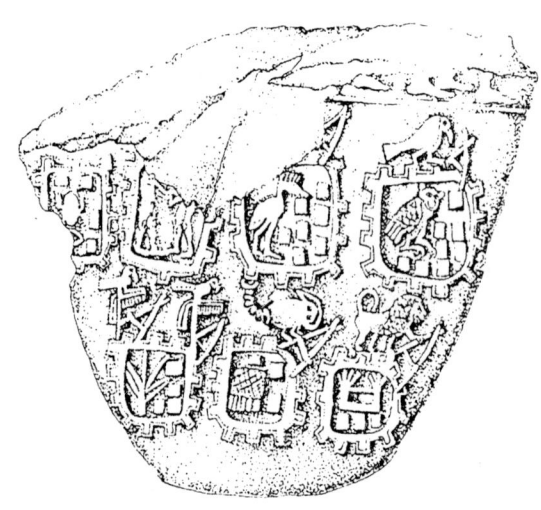

The Libyan Palette
(Drawings by Alicia Meza)

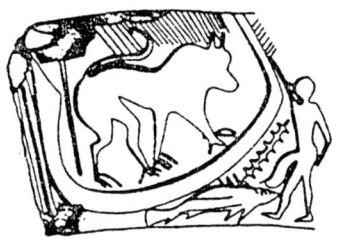 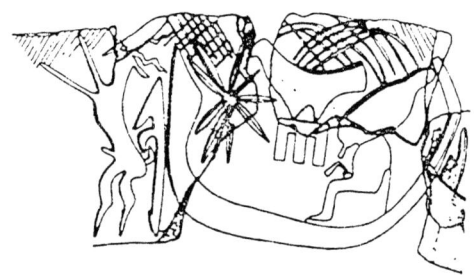
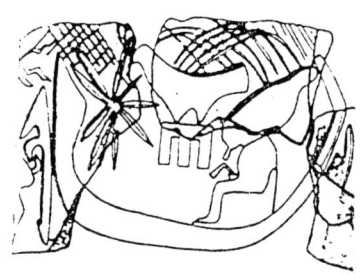 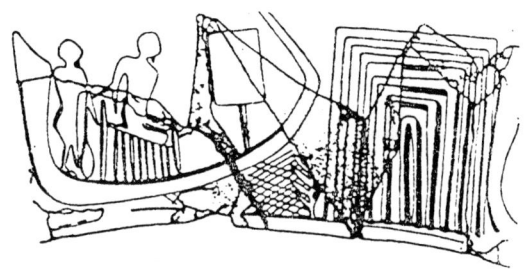

The Qustul Incense Burners
(Drawings by Alicia Meza)

relationships that involve decision making there is always the element of unpredictability that escapes planning and programming.

The causes for the development of social complexity are multiple, and the exact combination and proportion in which stochastic forces merged to create the proper environment for state formation, perhaps, will never be known. However, we can study the theoretical framework in which these events may have occurred, the road for future research being open to further improvement in archaeological regional analysis interpretation (Johnson, 1977: 479, 501-02).

As stated by Professor Conant (Nov. 1993 classes), seeing people in context–a great contribution made by Herschkowitz to Anthropology–is important to appreciate cultural changes through space and time. Egypt had the privileged geographical position of being within a diverse cultural context, not only African but also Mediterranean and southwestern Asian. Perhaps this privileged position in such diverse cultural context was the catalytic ingredient that made Egypt such an exceptional and unique civilization.

Chapter Two

Regional Description and Historical Information

The two regions of the Nile and the Tigris-Euphrates valleys are extensive and circumscribed; they also are rich in silt and agricultural potential. Within these two valley areas, centers of high population density developed during early prehistoric times. Both areas shared the blessing and the burden of floodwaters which brought in life to their inhabitants but which sometimes meant destruction and death.

The Nile Valley's floodplain was wider and richer than the one in the Tigris-Euphrates Valley, and the annual floodwaters were more predictable and easier to control in Egypt than in Mesopotamia (Trigger, 1983:13-15). Along the river bank and reaching among the hills near the Theban plateau, natural irrigation basins where the waters were retained provided an ideal ground for cultivation among the levees on which people could dwell all year-around. Rainfall also favored the agricultural potential of the land, and even the wadis among the foothills were fertile pastureland.

Life was not so easy in the Delta, where the inhabitants had to adapt to a continuous change of landscape because the branches of the Nile tended to switch courses and the settlements had to be built on natural mounds or "gezirat" that rose up to six meters above the floodplain. These watercourses' changes sometimes produced an increase in settlement area, developing centers where the watercourses met, for instance, at Buto, Tanis, Mendes, and Abusir (Bietak, 1979:97).

The general settings of Egypt and Mesopotamia were even more different than their river valleys. Mesopotamia was flanked by a series of highly diversified altitudes, rainfall patterns, and distribution of vegetation that

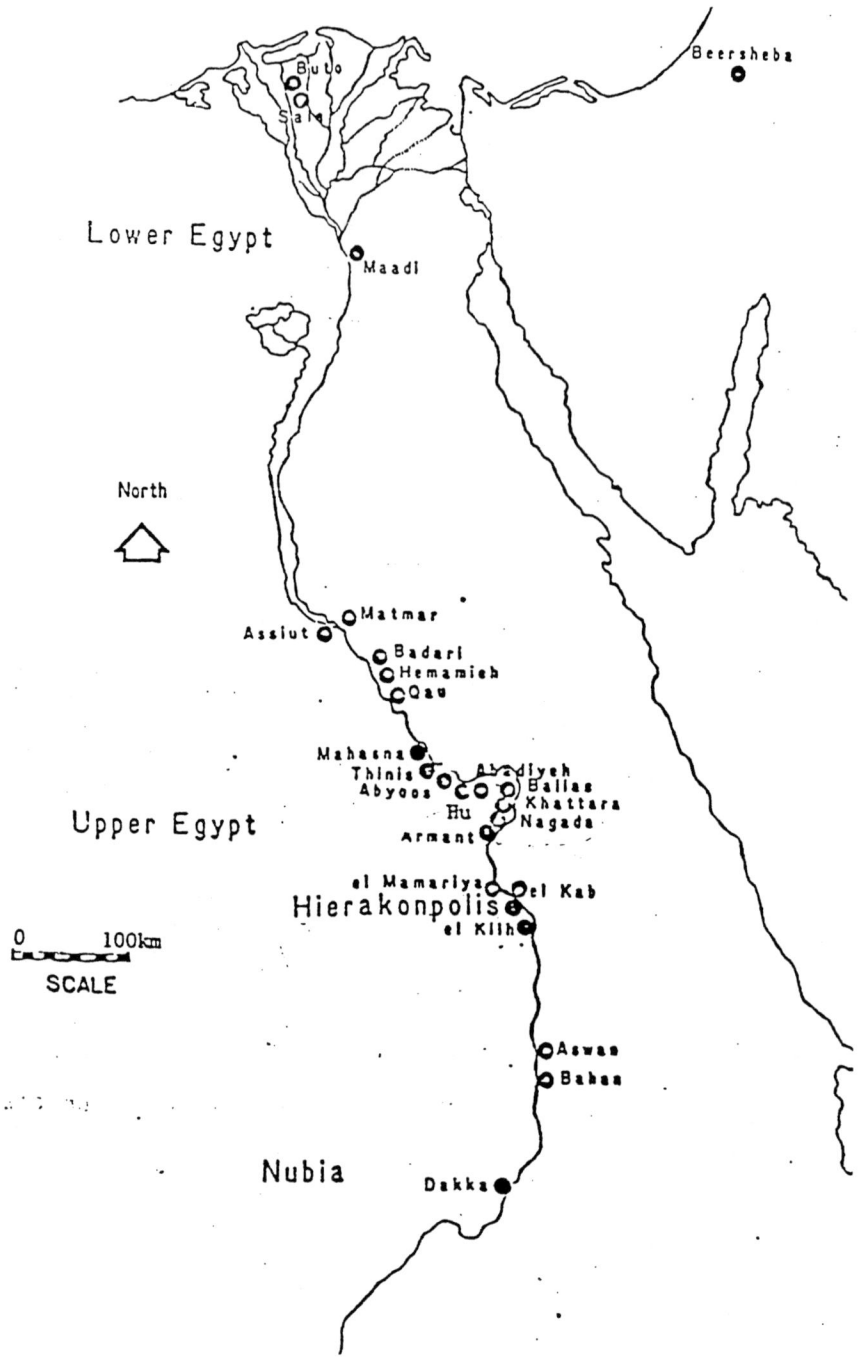

witnessed the earliest development of sedentary agricultural life. Such diversity encouraged trade, communications, and innovations in subsistence patterns (Trigger, 1983:14). Instead, the Nile Valley's relative isolation and predictable flooding patterns provided a more confident and highly differentiated way of life for its inhabitants, which differed from that of neighboring countries.

The Egyptian Prehistoric Towns

Egyptian prehistoric towns proliferated along the Nile valley, all the way from the Delta to Nubia. Some of these towns, such as Abydos and Hierakonpolis in Upper Egypt, acquired great importance. Abydos was an area consisting of settlements and cemeteries. Great enclosures were discovered there by Mariette and Petrie and early dynastic ivory labels were uncovered within a mastaba attributed to Queen Merneith of the First Dynasty. The enclosure of King Aha, also belonging to the same dynasty, resembled the paneled walls found in cult places and depicted on the Libyan palette.[2] The early excavators also unearthed, mostly in royal burials, wine jars with incised pot-marks. Further excavations done by Gunther Dreyer in Abydos have uncovered possible tokens and tags with phonetic writing MDKI (1998) V. 86, and still many more of these incised wine jars dating from the Late Predynastic Period (Naqada III) (1993:10). Most of these objects are in the Museum of The University College, London and in the Museum at Zagazig in Egypt.

William A. Griswold, using grave volume and statistical functions, examined social stratification in Armant. This settlement became an important Predynastic town on the west bank of the Nile, south of Abydos and the modern city of Luxor. Armant has also been researched by several scholars such as Kathryn Bard, who examined and analyzed its social stratification during the fourth millennium B.C. Bard used cluster analysis for the examination of social stratification. Griswold's data agrees with Bard's conclusion that there was evidence of a ranked society at an early Predynastic date at Armant. Bard based her assessment on Pebbles and Kus' criteria for establishing a mortuary patterning. She examined children's treatment after death for "ascribed" versus "achieved" social status and used ivory tags, rare materials, and energy expended in constructing and provisioning of the graves as status markers (Griswold, 1992:193-98).[3]

Griswold also agrees with Bard that social stratification in Armant did not achieve a complexity beyond a ranked society. Contrary to what was expected, increasing inequality did not go along with the increase of average grave volume throughout time. The reasons for this unpredictable contradiction may have been Armant's geographical position between two centers of developing political and probably military power, such as Naqada and Hierakonpolic (196 and footnotes). This observation agrees with one proposed by Johnson on the causes for collapse in the Susiana plains during the late Uruk period when a similar situation may have occurred with Uruk's expansion and the subsequent loss of power and population in centers, such as Choga Mish and Susa (1988-89:9-15). Johnson, though hints at the possibility that these events were two independent processes (Johnson, personal communication).

Armant, at its early stage of social stratification when power and control were at an incipient level, experienced its highest level of inequality. Later, when power and social stratification developed at Naqada and Hierakonpolis, Armant's position began to be overshadowed, perhaps because the Armant elites were moving out and into these two new centers, looking for new opportunities and choices for production and consumption.

During the beginning of the Dynastic period, Armant began to grow again in complexity. However, the cause of this increasing inequality seems to have been not the increase of individual inequality but, perhaps, a royal imposition ordered by the administrative hierarchy to create elites to satisfy the crown's own need for support (Griswold, 1992:197 and footnote).

Burials at the Badarian areas presented evidence of social inequality in Middle Egypt during early Predynastic times. Kathryn Bard did a quantitative analysis on burials at Armant and Naqada, and she believed that the Badarian period preceded the Amratian time at El Khatara at around 3700 B.C. (Anderson, 1992:51-66; Bard, 1987:). This Badarian culture was also located by Caton-Thompson at Hammamieth, where eighteen cemeteries were analyzed in the east bank of the Nile and in the Matmar, Mostagedda, and Badari regions with 725 burials (Brunton and Caton-Thompson, 1928: 69-88). By analyzing all grave goods, Guy Brunton also found that these goods were not distributed at random because there was an association between grave goods and grave area, grave goods and grave condition, and grave goods and age status of grave occupant. However, there was no association between grave goods and the sex of the grave occupant. Larger graves had more goods, and sub-adults had more goods than adults because age status was associated with grave goods. House burials were reserved for children; adults were buried in cemeteries. Grave goods contained imports, such as Red Sea shells, carnelian beads, and malachite. There were four types of burials: burials with exotic goods and non-utilitarian objects, wealthy burials with used articles such as cosmetic palettes or ivory vases, burials similar to wealthy burials but with local materials, and burials with used domestic materials (Anderson, 1992:53-66).

This difference in burials implied different access to resources. Also, the location of burials was related to status. For instance, the more wealthy were located at the eastern cemetery with ivory and carnelian goods, which were clustered in specific areas. Among men adults there were bead belts that perhaps indicated authority. Although the analysis of data suggests a bimodal dispersion of goods, wealthy and non-wealthy, associated with the social division of Badarian population, social complexity seemed limited here.

Other objects, described by Brunton as "ear-stubs" or "stoppers," are marked with a "nn." The pierced disks were found not only in Badarian graves but in Amaratian burials as well in sites such as Mahasna, Abydos, and Nagada. These objects were made of clay and also marked "nn," but Brunton failed to give them an utilitarian purpose because they are listed as "doubtful."[4] Pot-marks other than this occur in Amratian sherds and in small objects of clay which are strung together and are similar to the strung tokens of Schmandt-Besserat's corpus.

Buto, a town in the Delta and known in ancient Egyptian texts as Dep, was analyzed by Thomas Van der Way (1992:217-26), who has done extensive research and excavation work in this site with the Gewan Archaeological Institute in Cairo. According to ancient Egyptian tradition, this city was the counterpart, as a religious center, of Hierakinpolis in Upper Egypt. Buto is a settlement that should go back to the fourth millennium B.C. Work initiated by the Gewan Institute revealed there two meters in depth layer of Lower Egyptian culture, followed by layers of Naqada culture. The Lower Egyptian culture belonged to a complex called the Buto-Maadi culture and these two layers corresponded to Naqada I, II, IIc and IId and continued until Dynasty 0. The major group of finds consists of twelve finger-like clay objects slightly thicker at one end than at the other; all have circular-cross sections and look like delicate clay nails smoothed and rolled before having been fired to a hard consistency. Two of the objects have incisions made with a pointed tool, their color is reddish-brown and red and grayish-brown. Although the archaeologist's report does not indicate any use for this type of artifacts, he speculates that the nails may have been used as decorating mosaic, such as those used in Mesopotamia. The objects were hollowed and incised and there is the possibility they were used as envelopes to contain tokens. Nevertheless, von der Way does acknowledge the fact that the nails are similar to the mosaic nails from Uruk.[5] This similarity is evidence of personal contact between people from Mesopotamia and Buto which was being influenced by Mesopotamian architectonic style; for instance, the Naqada IIb period may have corresponded to the period of Uruk VIII to VI. At Habuba Kabira in Syria, a piece of Egyptian N-ware was found that was used in Egypt during the Naqada Iib period. These finds may have been part of a trade network of stations along the Balik, Habur, and Upper Euphrates (von der Way, 1992:220, and footnote No. 11). This network of colonies and long distance trade are no longer attested during the late Uruk period and Jemdet-Nasr period, according to Surenhagen, who suggests that these finds may correspond to the Middle Uruk period.[6]

These nails or cones, according to von der Way (220), were the product of the connections between Buto and Syria and may have occurred by sea since evidence is lacking for a Palestine contact. A sea link between Syria and Buto and other cities in the Delta may have facilitated Mesopotamian relationships with Egypt because these other Delta centers may have passed or traded the Mesopotamian goods to Upper Egypt during the Naqada time. Another possible sea link may have been the Arabian peninsula and across the Red Sea.

The Mesopotamian influence on Egyptian architecture is embedded in the niche recesses occurring in Egyptian Predynastic fortified walls, an influence that was in decline right after the First Dynasty. Kaiser reports that objects found in habitational quarters of the First Dynasty at Elephantine, in present day Aswan, were similar to those found at Buto. In the debris of the third millennium B.C. at Tell el Farkha in the eastern Delta, the same type of nails or cones were found. They were also used as funeral gifts at Helwan and at a mastaba at Dahla. These finds reveal that those objects were used in a systematic way throughout Egypt and that they may have been part of the mail system of the early Predynastic times.

Another important center, in the Delta, may have been the city of Sais where the type of building using niche recesses was probably influenced by simple models traced to the Ubaid period at the beginning of the fourth millennium B.C. of the temple of Eridu (von de Way, 1992).

According to Wenke and Brewer, the Fayum was one of the most occupied areas in Egypt from 7000-4000 B.C. It also was the earliest known site which presented evidence for agriculture in the Nile Valley. Nevertheless, soon after 4000 B.C., the site was nearly abandoned probably because it was less productive than other sites in the Valley. The site was reoccupied only in 300 B.C. with the Ptolomies when productivity was greatly increased by draining the lake. When Caton-Thompson excavated the south shore of the lake, she found artifacts similar to those of Hammamieth. However, the Fayum culture was more similar to that of Merimda Beni Salama and its ceramic tradition more similar to those ceramic traditions of the Delta cultures. Furthermore, one adaptation that was similar to both Fayum and Merimda were the cultigens found in both areas which were originally from southwest Asia and were introduced and adapted shortly before 5000 B.C. by both cultures. This southwest Asian adaptation was taken by the peoples from the western desert who had already developed their own economy based on their home resources. A site that, according to Wenke, presented early evidence for "the emergence of initial cultural complexity" at el Fayum was site FS-3, first excavated by Caton-Thompson. "These signs indicative of social development were population growth and the beginning of economic diversification and integration at Naqada, Hierakonpolis and other southern sites" (Wenke, 1992:177).

By 4000 B.C., the climate was becoming drier in northwest Africa and many people began moving toward the Nile Valley. At this time, the lithic industry at the Fayum became different from the lithics in Fayum A and more similar to those of Upper Egypt. By 3500 B.C. the lithic style of Maadi was similar to that of southwest Asia. Afterwards, the Fayum acquired a similar ceramic style to the Maadis, achieving in this way a fusion of Lower and Upper Egyptian Predynastic cultures.

At Giza, the Boston Museum excavated the site of Kafr Ghatti in 1958, where in tomb I there were intact in situ, some artifacts that appeared to be an envelope with its tokens. Reisner concluded that this tomb may have been from Dynasty 0-I, a time when Upper and Lower Egyptian tomb construction was becoming different from each other: deep underground rock-cut tombs evolved in the Memphis area and a corbel-roofed tomb type developed in Upper Egypt (Engles, 1990:71-88).

A master's thesis by Jeremy Geller (1984:1-22) on Hierakonpolis ceramic industry was correlated with Harlan's Ph.D. dissertation on Hierakonpolis settlement patterns. Predynastic sites in a major wadi three kilometers from the cultivation land were examined by Harlan, who believes that these sites flourished during the late Amratian and early Gerzean periods Naqada I, 4000-3500 B.C., and Naqada II, 3500-3200 B.C., respectively (1985:1-12). Two kinds of ware were examined: red ware associated with cemeteries and rough ware associated with habitational areas and craft semi-specialists and non-specialists. Harlan concluded the primary reason for Predynastic settlements at Hierakonpolis in Wadi Abul Suffian was cultural and not ecological as previously thought, meaning that the sites were related to mortuary activity rather than to farming activities favored by an increased rainfall. Harlan concluded the settlements also had a centralized ceramic production and a high degree of specialization with complex settlement patterning (235-42). These observations were based on the ceramics' standardized dimensions, that were an indication of mass production and craft specialization—both elements concomitant with incipient social complexity (Johnson, 1977:485-94).

Fairsevis' excavations in Hierakonpolis yielded objects of diverse shapes that were classified in the field report as "of an unidentified use" (1971-1972:12-13). In effect, these objects appear to be perforated, incised tokens (Appendix 1-6).

Matmar was another site of the Tasian and Badarian cultures that provided evidence of foreign contacts. This site was a four-mile stretch of land located in Upper Egypt near the site of Badari. Brunton, after observing diverse objects made of non-local raw materials such as turquoise and copper, concluded that not only the raw materials were of a foreign origin, but the manufactured stone vases and steatite beads were coming from "a district not far removed from Matmar, where there existed a culture in a much higher degree of development" (1937:2-12). Among the objects from these Predynastic graves were cylinders and labels with incisions filled with a black paste and rosettes made of ivory filled with lapis lazuli. Pot-marks were done before firing and some of them, such as a bull with long horns, were similar to those found at El Amrah. There also were tags with holes to pass through leather thongs and other perforated objects that looked like tokens (fig. 3).

Kaiser and Payne did a chronology of Naqada based on geographic distribution of grave goods; a mapping of these cemeteries was done before by Petrie (1901). Naqada was an important Predynastic center near Hierakonpolis that was first excavated by Petrie in 1895 (Petrie and Quibell, 1896). Kaiser (1957) reached a grave goods chronological order by examining the contents of tombs and correlating them with other Predynastic cemeteries in the area. Using these studies as a basis for his own investigation, Payne concluded that Naqada went throughout several stages of development according to its graves' wares. There was a transition in the dominant ware, from B ware to R ware to L ware. There also was a change in decorated typology. These sequences, when compared with the Armant sequences done by Kaiser, showed little variance between them. This sequences' variation may reflect the difference in the social development that may have occurred in both sites (1992:185-92). In spite of the difference indicated by Payne in ceramic variation sequence, Armant and Naqada were situated close enough to each other to have participated in the same regional system. Their geographical position have allowed a cultural interaction that may have subsequently resulted in similar cultural developments, such as ceramic variation.

Bodil Mortensen used carbon dating to do a chronology of el Omari, an important Predynastic site on the eastern side of the Nile and south of Cairo. The dates obtained by Mortensen were between 4500-4100 B.C., earlier than previously given dates. Only two other sites had comparable datings to el Omari: el Fayum in Middle Egypt and Merimda at the apex of the Delta. These last two sites had a change in settlement pattern produced by a change in climate that subsequently brought a change in ceramic tradition (1992:173-74). These three last sites were probably involved within the same interacting region system that provided information and cultural exchange among them.

Sumer and Elam

According to Nissen (1988), the systems that developed in southern Mesopotamia and Susiana in Iran also had considerable climatic changes during the beginning of the fourth millennium B.C. During this period, the climate became much drier and cooler, allowing for a series of ecological and socioeconomic changes in those areas. Since Lower Mesopotamia was located on the Euphrates-Tigris valley, a large part of that area was completely submerged under water before those climate changes occurred. During flooding time, the rivers became so swollen that the unsubmerged areas were being flooded as well. After the climatic conditions became drier,

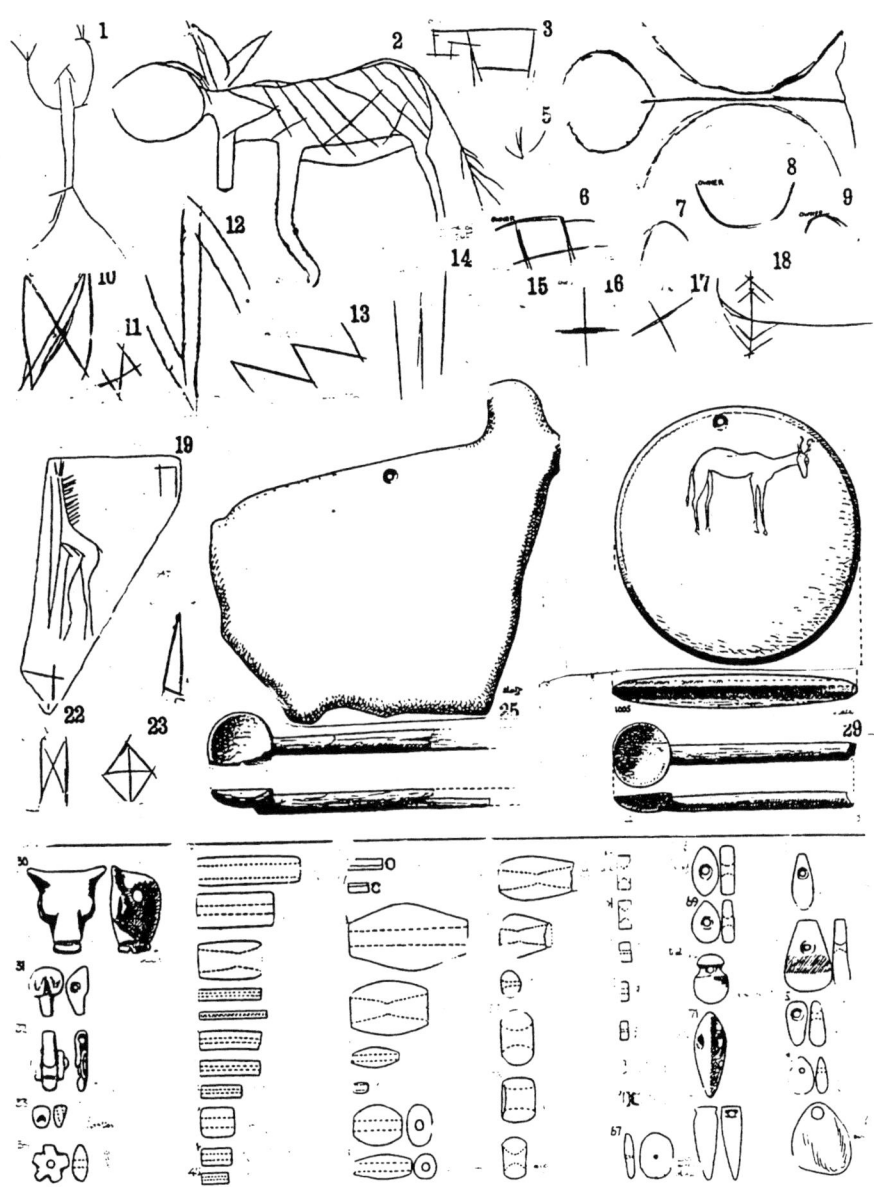

Matmar Tags and Perforated Objects
(Drawings by Alicia Meza)

the number of settlements in southern Mesopotamia suddenly increased. The sea level lowered and new ground was opened to more inhabitable circumstances and land cultivation (Johnson, classes of April 2-19, 1993).

The two areas of Uruk and Susa bared different regional developments that could be, in part, explained by the difference in water availability those areas had after the change in their climatic conditions (Nissen, 1988:58-66). Precipitation was differentially in both areas and this scarcity of water didn't guarantee continued plant cultivation in the Uruk area, which developed later than that of Susiana. Although Susa developed earlier, Uruk with time achieved a highly stratified society with a differentiated economy. This social development agrees with the development of complex tokens because these types of devices first appeared in Uruk (Schmandt-Besserat, 1992:36-39).

During the last half of the fourth millenium B.C., much of Greater Mesopotamia had unprecedented social and cultural developments that eventually led to social complexity and the formation of the first state systems in those areas. After the Ubaid during the Terminal Susa A period in 3900 B.C., settlements in southwestern Iran reorganized again, after which appears to had been a collapse of a chiefdom in the area (Johnson, 1980). Eventually, during the Middle Uruk period 3400 B.C., three large centers developed with Susa being the largest. It is at this time when the first state formation in that area appears to have been consolidated.[7]

Meanwhile, in Sumer, Uruk also was growing as a center that later became the head of the settlement system, amounting to about 382 ha of aggregate occupation, and which consolidated into a pristine state (Johnson, 1988-1989:1-3). During the Uruk expansion, similar Uruk ceramic assemblages, architectural style, and administrative technology spread to other areas such as southwestern Iran and the Upper Euphrates in Syria (1-3). The Susiana system during the late Uruk period 3200 B.C. seems to have been participating in a major interregional system with great movements of people from one center to another. These events coincided with the development of a more complex system of markings and the eventual innovation of writing in Mesopotamia and in Egypt. Long-range trade of raw materials that were not locally originated also were detected in the archaeological records of both Egypt and Mesopotamia.

Chapter Three

Discussion of Token's Role in Mesopotamia

Plain tokens without any incisions or marks first appeared between 8000 and 7500 B.C. in sites in Syria and Iran. This simple system of counting became more elaborate with the passing of time, and another system of complex tokens was introduced to improve counting.[8] Complex tokens were more elaborate and were extensively incised with more variety of markings. They began appearing about 4400 B.C. at centers such as Uruk in southern Mesopotamia, Susa in Elam, and Habuba Kabira in Syria Schmandt-Besserat (1992:19-50).

Simple and Complex Tokens

Generally, tokens were made of clay and fired after being shaped. They also were made of other materials such as stone, bitumen, and even plaster (29)[9] Later, during the third to the second millennium B.C., tokens reverted to being plain again; this type of token was found as far as Ain Ghazal, Beida, Jericho, and Meggido.

Some sites produced great quantities of tokens, such as Jarmo, Iraq, where two thousand tokens were found, while at Uruk 800 complex tokens were uncovered near the sanctuary of Eanna (late Uruk period 3500-3100 B.C.). Temples and structures associated with storage and reckoning of goods were the sites to produce most of the complex tokens assemblages. Other types of assemblages were those associated with funerary deposits, such as at Tell es-Sawwan, although this is rare (101:172).

The temple of Eanna's evolution since the time of its foundation in the late Ubaid period, 4500-4200 B.C., to its transformation into a prestigious temple in the Middle Uruk period, 3800-3500 B.C., presents evidence for Uruk's social development. Plain tokens were found in the earliest levels of this temple, which yielded only small assemblages of them. During the late Uruk period, when the temple was in its most prestigious stage, the largest assemblage of complex tokens was uncovered. Evidence for record keeping and writing on clay tablets done with reeds was found at level IV of the temple (59-72).

Although complex tokens appear later at Susa than at Uruk, Susa in Elam presented the second largest collection of tokens next to Uruk. Near Susa's Acropolis, 780 tokens were found similar to those of Uruk (4000 B.C.). Meanwhile, at Habuba Kabira the appearance of tokens is parallel with that of Uruk and Susa (182). The later date for Susa complex tokens, which is at the time of its state formation (178), confirms the tokens' origin as being Mesopotamian (198-99). Nevertheless, the beginning of tokens coincides with food production since the need for counting and accounting was related to agriculture or the demographic and socio-political changes it implies. For instance, the excavation at Mureybet, Syria (177-78) indicated the tokens' association with reckoning, cultivation, and storage. Although tokens are not being related to trade, later on they also served this need.

Although evidence coming from Mesopotamian tombs is scarce, one striking feature of graves containing tokens is the presence of lavish furniture or exotic and luxurious items such as gold ornaments, alabaster vessels, dentalia shells, or carnleian beads and obsidian as in tomb 107 at Tepe Gaura (171). Serpentine and electrum vessels as well as gold rosettes, beads, stone mace-heads, and lapis lazuli also were found at Tell El Sawan (171-72).

Evolution of Tokens into Signs

Tokens were secured in envelopes bearing seals of authority and markings or notations. Tablets also bore signs or notations for containers.[10] The patterns illustrated on seals were rosettes, lines of rams, goats or cattle, and snakes or monsters in heraldic posture, motifs that are all found in the art style of Egyptian ceramics during the Naqada period, 4000 B.C. War scenes with kings besieging cities and prisoners being taken away, also were depicted in seals and tablets (180-82). Impressed tablets were a transitional phase from pictography or graphic representation of tokens to pictographic writing since some impressed signs were supplanted by pictographs traced with a sharp stylus. For instance, oval or triangular signs evolved into incised pictographs, while other signs became impressed incised; wedges and circular signs remained impressed, creating a dichotomy between two kinds of scripts: impressed and pictographic (139). These tablets were a decisive transition to the invention of writing.

Some type of tokens more common throughout the Near East may have evolved into specific impressed signs because sigh impression was the most ancient and the most rudimentary of the two early forms of writing. For instance, cones and cylinders or disks and spheres may have turned into wedges or circular signs (142).[11] A result of this association is that signs were identified by the context rather than by their shape.

For instance, short and long wedges representing cones and cylinders were distinguished by their position on the tablet: long wedges next to the edge, long ones at the center of the tablet (142). This derivation of circular signs from spheres and lenticular disks can be set apart by their association with other signs, such as short wedges associated with spheres and long wedges with lenticular disks. On the other hand, notched spheres and incised triangles were prototypes for impressed/incised signs which attest to the close relationship between impressed and incised signs, the last step of the evolution from tokens to writing (142). The next step of this evolution was the conversion of impressed signs and markings into incised pictographs, such as ovoids, pinched spheres, plain ovoids, and plain triangles which can be matched to specific signs (fig. 1-2 in the appendix). In this way an association of tokens and signs can be made with meaning of the derived cuneiform signs: tokens tetrahedrons may have represented units of labor and Schmandt-Besserat correlates them to two triangular signs identified as "temple servant" or "dua" which means "build, make, construct." Dockets meaning wages earned for services were to be exchanged by rations of barley and may have been modeled in clay in the shape of tetrahedrons. Labor or manpower was in this manner treated as a commodity and still is today in the Middle East. Some tokens identified by pictographs stood for units of merchandise, and the difference between the use of plain and complex tokens was that complex tokens showed greater precision of information, such as the species, sex, and age of the animals labeled (152-54). During the fourth millennium B.C., tokens also stood for finished products, such as bread, oil, perfume, wool, metal bracelets, and cloth.

Tokens in Context

Although the invention and the development of simple tokens into complex tokens was not related to trade, later they were used for this purpose. For instance, evidence for this idea is the raw materials found at Uruk that were not related to the number of tokens found there. Nevertheless, the Uruk temple was probably involved in securing goods from distant markets, in spite of not reflecting these facts in its records since many raw materials and goods were of a foreign origin, such as alabaster, obsidian, and lapis lazuli Schmandt-Besserat (167-68).

Impressed and pictographic tablets continued to deal with the same kinds of goods as the token system and with the same quantities, showing that writing was not indebted to any visible change in the economy; however, the economy played a role in the development of the token system. Although trade was indirectly involved in the invention of tallies, there is no evidence for commerce and tablets until the third millennium B.C. The meaning of tokens found in graves or in impressive buildings may have been symbolic of rations of food as offerings for eternity, although this is doubtful because tokens are not found in all burials. Moreover, food offerings in burials are not a common Mesopotamian feature but are Egyptian. Perhaps, the tokens' presence in impressive and luxurious Mesopotamian graves, such as tombs 102, 110, and 114 at Tepe Gawra, was to confer prestige to the elites since tokens were found along with rich materials and goods, such as gold, serpentine, and obsidian, and electrum vessels and gold beads (171-72).

It seems that pictographic tablets and tokens belonged to the temple bureaucracy of the third millennium B.C., such as the Eanna precinct. It is assumed that both devices, tokens and tablets, fulfilled the same accounting function since they had the same content and belonged to the same context. Moreover, the art and cuneiform texts of 3000 B.C. suggest that Sumer had a distributive economy involving the temples, the elite which administered the communal property, and the commons who provided the surplus goods to the temple. This distributive system relied upon a system of reckoning and recordkeeping: a vital function provided by the tokens and tablets systems. The Sumerian redistributive system may have developed in the temple of Eanna, and it must have drawn its origin from prehistoric antecedents. Plain tokens of the eighth millennium B.C. "...made possible the rise of a ranked society, preparing the background for the powerful fourth to third millennium bureaucracy" (Schmandt-Besserat 177-78). The political power that developed out of and which was based on the development of reckoning technology could not have occurred without it. Still, the rise of monumental architecture which necessitated large amounts of expending for materials, construction, and adornment denotes a quantum jump in the quantity of resources available to the community; therefore, the temple of Eanna suggests a taxation system which meant a new way of pooling surpluses. Taxation presupposes enforcement and coercion for collection. This was manifested in the use of beveled-rim bowls for rationing which according to Beale (1978:310), also were used for offerings. In Susa their appearance coincided with the destruction of the temple when the buildings were replaced by more modest structures. This collapse meant a conquest and a break between the two cultures since Sumerian pictographic writing never penetrated Susa. A possible southern domination of Elam is further supported by seals picturing warfare.[12]

The distribution of complex tokens in Elam also attests to its incipient social complexity since in Elam three sites had had complex tokens: Susa, which was a city, Choga Mish, a town, and tow other lesser centers such as Ks54 (178-80). This social system presents, as demonstrated by Johnson (1973:101-102), four levels of social organization with three levels of administration, an indication of pristine state formation.

Another aspect of the tokens' importance in the development of writing is the development of the counting system. Mesopotamian and Sumerian numeration systems at the beginning were just a "three-count" system after which "many" was the earliest description for more than "three." Three also was the morphene for plural, which also was used in Egyptian writing (Gardiner 1982:58). This three-count system was hard to overcome in Mesopotamia where the first numerals emerged in Uruk IV about 3100 B.C., and they were signs encoding the concept of oneness, twoness, and threeness abstracted for any particular entity. Thus, two systems developed numerals for abstract numbers and pictographs for commodities. Tokens dealt with concrete counting and the pictograph tablets with abstract counting. These first pictographic tablets could express more than one unit and more than the number "three" since they dealt with abstract entities, and they consisted of impressed signs. Goods were expressed by incised pictographs. For instance, a circle with a cross for sheep with five wedges for the number five (Schmandt-Besserat 195-96). This is the first evidence for the creation of modern arithmetic.

Chapter Four

Discussion of Tokens and Graffiti Pot-marks

The invention of writing has always been linked to the emergence of the first state systems. Perhaps this linkage is due to the fact that writing was always found in sites where social complexity was already under way, if not completely achieved. Probably the anomaly of this assumption is that there were states which, even though they were accepted as such, like the Inca state, they never developed a writing system. However, these two elements in socio-cultural history, state formation and writing, seem to have been intertwined with each other. Sometimes it has been speculated whether writing helped state formation. The truth is writing was based in more rudimentary systems of conveying information in an abstract way. Moreover, state formation can be demonstrated to have existed along with those abstract communication systems developed before writing and to which writing owes its origins.

There is no question about the millennium in which the first state formation systems occurred in the Mesopotamian world. Although dates are relative, the fourth millennium B.C. saw the emergence of Susa and Warka as centers of those systems. The millennium for the emergence of the Egyptian state is more or less accepted as also the fourth, but I think Egypt has been shortchanged about in which portion of the fourth millennium B.C. state formation occurred. Moreover, as reported in the last chapter, at the time when Elam and Sumer witnessed their first states this was also the time when the counting and communication system were being developed from tokens to impressed tablets which presented a way to convey information by markings. These markings also were used to identify merchandise, ownership, and provenance of goods. In Egypt this system of markings has been found in Predynastic pots, labels, and seals of Dynasty 0 (Bard, 1992:304). Although the Egyptian evidence is more tenuous than the Mesopotamian one, nevertheless it is still abundant enough to have been, in part, consolidated in a corpus by Petrie (1896). The origin of Egyptian writing also has been the subject of several studies (Fairsevis, 1983; Arnett, 1982; Bard, 1992; Fischer, 1990). Some of these scholars have hinted at the possibility of Mesopotamian influence in the development of Egyptian writing. Others have hinted at the possibility that this invention contributed to state formation in Egypt. But there has not been an attempt to coordinate and correlate all the data. This attempt will be made here, beginning with a look first at the Egyptian case.

Egypt, the State and the Graffiti Pot-marks

Kathryn Bard did a study on the origins of Egyptian writing (1992:297). Royal writing may have been one of the consequences of state formation since its invention and use may have helped to legitimize an early unstable state. Her conclusions are based on the fact that early Egyptian proto-states may have formed by Naqa II or 3500 B.C. Nevertheless, the state in Egypt may have been achieved by the end of the Predynastic Period, a time of instability and during which writing may have served the function of legitimizing the new regime. Writing also may have served an economic function as well, developing three kinds of uses: royal seals, pot-marks, and jar sealings; combination of hieroglyphs and graffiti to convey messages; and royal commemorative art to legitimize the king's rule. These three points corroborate Baine's assumption that "the stimulus to create writing predates state formation and must be seen as part of the society cognitive and economic changes that occur as a society becomes more complex" (Baines, 1988:193, qd. In Bard, 1992:299).[13] Mud sealings similar to the Mesopotamian dating from Dynasty 0 proto-signs and tags on jars found at Abydos by Dreyer (1998) have prompted him to say the expansion and consolidation of the Egyptian state may have occurred before Dynasty 0 with an increasing administration using writing to help to order and control. Bard thinks, contrary to Fairsevis' assertions, decorated ware is not the precursor of writing since this developed as an affiliation of writing with pictorial art (301). For Bard writing was used as an additional specific pictorial message, while elaborate and general pictorial representation and symbolism was not writing (301). Bard adds that hieroglyphs of Dynasty 0 were used to caption political information portrayed pictorially with writing, specifying the meaning of graphic art, and that contra Baines, who asserts writing needed representation to explain statements and ideology, hieroglyphic signs are part of an elaborate system representing a compelling centralization and power of the king (301).

In spite of Bard's assertions that pot-marks may not have been connected to hieroglyph's development, Emery (1961:198-201) indicates inscribed ivory and wood labels were used not only to mark commodities but also to mark on them the name of the king, year, and reign. During the First Dynasty, there were in use jar sealings and other objects inscribed, such as certain "gaming pieces" from which 203 hieroglyphs were later used during the Old Kingdom language. These marks on pots were made with a sharp instrument before firing. A system of marking used all over Egypt for more than three hundred years, these pot-marks were listed by various excavators, such as Petrie at Tarkhan, de Morgan at Naqada, and Cecil Firth at North Saqqara (202). Emery also indicates this system of marking commodities was related to the one used in Mesopotamia, as it is indicated by Mesopotamian cylinder seals dating from Jamdet el Nasr period, 3100-2900 B.C., found in Egypt (30-40).

The Red Sea route may have been used for a long-range trade between Egypt and Mesopotamia. However, the Delta area also provided information about a more probable route between the two areas: Palestine and the Simai. Emery explains that there is a record on labels found at Abydos from Naqada of the building of a temple in Sais by King Narmer and of the founding of Memphis (51). In Saqqara, Emery also found many small objects and small pottery jars with painted inscriptions. The labels from Abydos also record the visit of King Zer from the First Dynasty to Buto and Sais. Among the records from Nubia at Wadi Halfa there is a rock inscription on the west bank of the Nile depicting King Zer with his bound enemies. A collection of jewelry from the same site is in the Toronto Museum, an indication of an already sophisticated society which supported craft specialists. During the reign of King Peribsen, the followers of Seth, opposed to the followers of Horus, from the previous reigns are mentioned in the records. They also mention the cult of Osiris in Busiris, a town in the Delta (96-123). This fact is interesting since towns with fortified walls, such as those of the First Dynasty at Abydos and Hierakonpolis, are shown in the Libyan palette depicting the so-called Libyan campaign. The architecture of these walls was similar to Mesopotamian temple-wall architecture, using the same brick size in their construction (153-77). Although most of the evidence provided above is late, for the purposes of this study it is important because it demonstrates that markings on objects were later related to hieroglyphs; there are objects described as "gaming pieces" which are marked and look like tokens; there is a relationship between those objects, their marks, and Mesopotamia; and the evidence comes both from Upper and Lower Egypt, showing there were two possible routes of connection, which is also attested in brick-wall construction similar to the Mesopotamian style.

The importance of the Delta towns is their influence not only on Egyptian politics, but also on its ideology since Busiris is portrayed as the place of origin for the God Osiris. The Gods Horus and Seth also may have originated in a Delta town; therein, the followers of Horus and the followers of Seth, later identified with the king's ancestors souls, were probably ancient chiefs or kings from those towns or cities.

Among the artifacts found by Emery at Saqqara, some of them described as "gaming pieces" (fig. 4) that, in effect, are identical to tokens and bullas described in Schmandt-Besserat's corpus. Emery was not the only archaeologist to have related all these facts to the exchange relations between Mesopotamia and Egypt. Dominique Collon (1987:16), in a study on cylinder seals, indicates that they bear witness to trade relations between Susa, Syria, and Egypt. Collon believes the routes for such trade were via the Persian Gulf and around the Arabian peninsula and overland to the Mediterranean sea. Collon demonstrates that the Mesopotamian art motifs from Susa also are found in Predynastic and Dynastic palettes and knife handles from Egypt as well as in the architectural style of wall construction. While writing developed during this time, the art patterns used on Egyptian ceramics were similar to those used in Mesopotamia. These patterns were based on rows of standing animals and executed with a drill similar to those used for stamp seals. These designs found at Diyala, north of Baghdad, and from Syria and Susa to Egypt, are a clear indicative of exchange for Collon, who explains that, for instance, lapis lazuli was usually exchanged for gold throughout the Middle East as it is attested in the archaeological record (135).

Fairsevis excavated the site of Hierakonpolis for a long time, and he also proposed pot-marks as a possible origin for the Egyptian hieroglyphs. He observed that sites from Amratian and Gerzean times had a continuous occupation, and they had a great deposition of graffiti-inscribed pot-sherds with more concentration on the Gerzean sites (1983:1-6). Based on this observation, Fairsevis speculated an abstract symbolic system had already evolved at this time. This observation coincides with the results of the research on the Mesopotamian writing system done by Schmandt-Besserat. The importance of this coincidence is that Fairsevis denotes graffiti is not confined to just one site, such as Hierakonpolis but is found in other Egyptian Predynastic sites as well (5).

Fairsevis observed that the problem in dealing with early state formation in Egyptian archaeology is that all the Predynastic sites have been treated as being of a homogeneous culture, such as Naqada, if they presented similar ceramic decoration, a problem that originated with the seriology system used to classify them.[14]

Fairsevis presented a list of Egyptian Predynastic towns where selected graffiti occurred, indicating the diverse marks. There also is a series of conventional motifs found on Class D ware. A table showing the possible evolution of graffiti into hieroglyphs also is provided within the text (22-31). The basis for this correlation has been Gardiner's sign list (1982).

Arnett (1982) also has examined the Predynastic pot-marks and asserts that these marks expressed ideas of ownership or property and were early

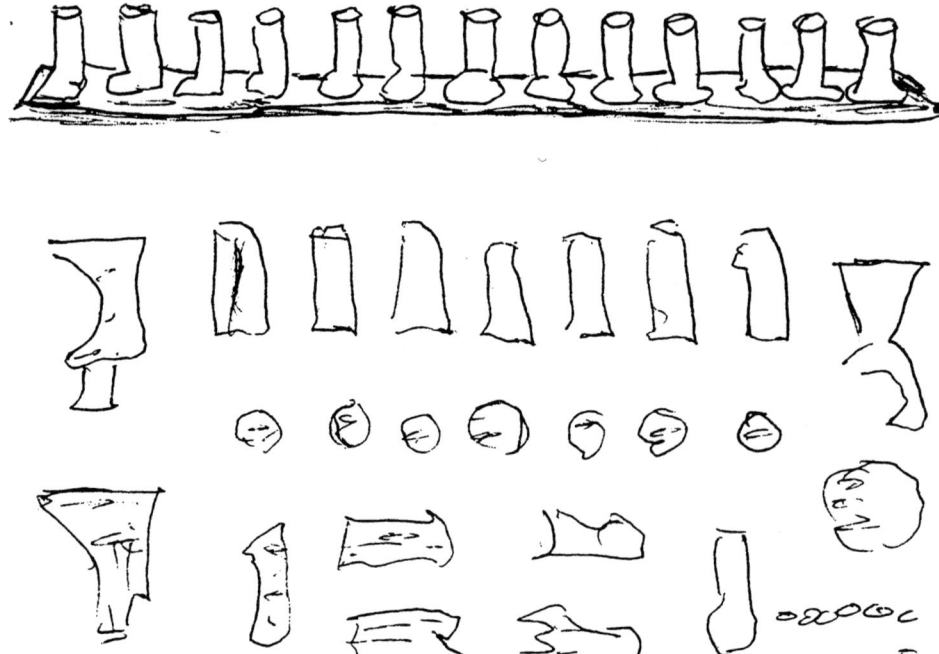

Gaming Pieces from Saqqara
(Drawings by Alicia Meza)

means by which these ideas were later formalized in hieroglyphic forms (1-6). Pot-marks, such as the "potted plant" from Deer el Tasa presented a fan-like appearance, later became the hieroglyph for the words "tree" or "fan" G.M 1. A figure similar to the hieroglyph for the word "libation," with a zigzag line projecting from a pot, later was found in the hieroglyph for the word "vomiting" G.D 26, depicted as lips with liquid moving away from them. The hieroglyph G.N 35 for "water" was depicted with a wavy line and the "niwt" sign meaning G.O 49 "town" or "city" was already depicted in very early painted tokens from Mesopotamia, the meaning there unknown. In Gardiner's sign list, the loaf of bread is represented to mean the letter "t," the sandy hill "k," the reed flower the "i," the square "p," the mouth "r," the placenta "h," and the reed shelter "h," (7-21). Also, according to Arnett, in Predynastic art there are carvings and figures in the round or relief that seem rudimentary forms of hieroglyphs, such as hawks, flies, scorpions, scarabs, and plows (23-29). Meanwhile, carved palettes and mace-heads also were the beginning of monumental inscriptions to commemorate historical events (31-43). This data has been correlated with Schmandt-Besserat's data in the appendix (fig. 1-6) and will be discussed later at the end of this chapter.

According to Gibson (1987), cylinder seals found their way out of Mesopotamia to Egypt and were overwhelmingly replaced by the inscribed scarabs, which were preferred and cut as cylinder seals. Nissen also has indicated that stamp seals were earlier than the cylinder seals and that probably, as proposed by Porada, they were the byproduct of stone bowl manufacturing since they were probably carved out of the unused core that came off from manufactured stone vessels. These seals were important to detect social stratification since persons of higher rank, such as officials or nobility, were using them as a symbol of their power and social status. Gibson asserts whole political careers can be reconstructed through the study of different titles and the seals used. Institutions, palaces, and temples and their respective relationships also can be detected through seal study as well as hereditary offices: who sealed what, for whom, and who received these commodities. The sort of jars used, their correlation with sealed stoppers, and their commodities also are a source of information about social stratification.

Van den Brink (1992:265-75) did a study on "Thinite pot-marks," "Thinnis" or "This" was the ancient site of Abydos. A seal impression from "This" found at Hierakonpolis had inscribed on it the combination of two signs: "niwt" and "ntr," meaning "town" and "god," respectively. These signs also were found on wine jars from pit burials, incised in the wet clay with a sharp instrument before being fired; the same technique practiced in Mesopotamia on token and tablet-making. On Petrie's corpus of pot-marks, van den Brink observed that the marks appeared in a patterning of lines and dots applied on the "wine jars." This systematic patterning of arranging was done in groups of three signs with three different combinations, which also occurred in combinations of two, following a steady rate of combinations that may have represented a grammar. For instance, it contains all three attested double combinations. An upside down "U" is in Gardiner's sign list number G.V 20, meaning "mdw," "speech."

G.Q 3 means "p," "seat," "base," "shrine," and "stool covering," like G.O 30, O 44, meaning "iat," "office."

Some signs also appeared alone (appendix, fig. 1-2). Helck proposes that these pot-marks refer solely to individual workshops, an opposed view to van den Brink's who believes they belonged to administration centers which distributed the commodities. An interesting fact is that these marks also were found on imported foreign pottery and on Egyptian vessels. The only difference between the imported and the Egyptian vessels was that on the imported ceramics the firing was always done after marking. With the Egyptian ceramics, this was not always the case. Moreover, some mark groupings were found more often than others, indicating perhaps their provenance was from more important centers.

The Appendix I have correlated in a chart the Egyptian graffiti pot-marks from Fairsevis' chart of diverse Predynastic sites, such as Diaspolis Parva, Matmar, Gerzeh, Hierakonpolis, Naqada, Armant, Amrah, Mostagedda, Badari, Naga er Der, and Mahasna and from the corpus of incisions found on tokens as done by Schmandt-Besserat, who also proposes the relationship of these markings to later cuneiform signs and their meaning. As I correlated the marks, I also went a little further and tried to see if they were correlating to later hieroglyphs and their meaning. My hypothesis here for this correlation is that if people from two different areas, cultures, and languages had engaged in long-distance trade, they may have had a way to communicate and be able to understand each other. If this communication had to withstand a long distance as well as probably several middlemen or posts the markings on goods and containers had to be substantially clear and durable. If such markings had meaning for the Mesopotamians, they also may have conveyed certain similar meaning to the Egyptians.

The interesting result of this correlation is that there is a correspondence in similitude of marks and in meaning. The meaning, mostly goods, and some of them animals, makes sense if we think of them as possible commodities for exchange or trade, local or interregional. For instance, the commodities with similar signs in the ancient marks are perfume, oil, honey, grain, figs, cloth, sheep, cows, ewes, metal, and "build," "construction" meaning perhaps manpower and labor, a commodity that today is still valuable and exchanged in the Middle East.

The Egyptian towns grouped by sign occurrence, and, therefore, by certain commodities are all the Predynastic sites mentioned above, some of which were engaged more than others in dealing with certain commodity. For instance, all of the sites had the sign for "sheep," but only Naqada had the sign for "ewe." Naqada, Armant, Naga er Der, Diaspolis Parva, and

Amrah all had the sign for perfume. If we presume these cities and those of Mesopotamia were involved in trade with each other, some goods may have been more appealing than others to certain cities. Perhaps direct access to resources, or perhaps other influencing factors, such as distance or the need or the desire for acquisition of those goods, played an important role in the way the goods were distributed. Nevertheless, if during early Predynastic times these activities were taking place, this is an indication that, at that time, proto-writing was similar in both regions–in Mesopotamia and in Egypt–and that the system of communication was viable and easily understood by both societies. Moreover, in spite of differences in language, the semitic influence is undeniably in ancient Egyptian grammar. Although Egyptian language also had African roots, this similitude in written communication demonstrates that the language belonged to the Afro-Asiatic family. In the course of evolution throughout time, both systems of marks eventually developed into their respective indigenous expression of language, with some similarities remaining in both of them. However, the signs resulting from those marks in cuneiform and in hieroglyphs turned out to be different from each other.

Chapter Five

Discussion of the Archaeological Evidence

In the last two chapters I have submitted evidence for the possible development of the Mesopotamian writing system derived from a concrete reckoning device as proposed by Denise Schmandt-Besserat. I also have reviewed the literature which provides philological information about Egyptian Predynastic pot-marks, their possible relationship with the development of hieroglyphs and a possible Mesopotamian influence in this development.

In this chapter I will review the archaeological field reports and all archaeological literature pertaining to this study in respect to: evidence for early social complexity within the Egyptian Predynastic towns; evidence for early state formation in Mesopotamia; and a possible parallel time of social development in Egypt to that of Mesopotamia.

Michael Hoffman did a comprehensive study from the Qadan culture at Wadi el Halfa to Omari and Maadi, near Cairo, and el Fayum and Hierakonpolis, where he excavated for many years along with Professor Fairsevis. At Tushka, near Aswan, the Qadan culture flourished at about 10,000 B.C. Petrrie Reisner, Wendrox, and Williams worked at cemetery 117 in Jebel Sahaba, finding evidence that this culture had developed a highly sophisticated way of life as well as social stratification at a much earlier date than that of Dynasty I in Egypt (Williams, 1980:14-21; 1986).

Petrie's excavations at Naqada, Ballas, Abadiyeh, and Hu in tombs dating from 5000-4000 B.C. yielded objects that could be identified as painted tokens (Petrie, 1896, 1901). After Petrie, Morgan excavated at Naqada, uncovering the Amratian period of 4000-3500 B.C. F./W. Green excavated at Hierakonpolis, where he found the famous palettes with depictions resembling the art of ancient Sumer and Elam (Hoffman 1979:105-124). According to Green's notes, at the Museum of Natural History in New York, the palettes presented evidence for a possible Egyptian connection with Susa and Uruk during the fourth millennium B.C. Green describes the early Gerzean-painted tombs from Hierakonpolis, one of them was the spectacular painted tomb 100 depicting men dressed in strange costumes, some fighting and one holding back two animals in a motif typical of Iranian and Mesopotamian artistic style (125-135).

At Hammamieh, year 1975, Caton-Thompson excavated the Badarian sites finding hut circles resembling those of Maadi and Omari. A well stratified sequence showed the Badarian, Amratian, and Gerzean cultures were subsequent to each other, dating from 5000-3500 B.C. (136-42). At el Amrah, Petrie found a model house made of clay that exhibited a Dynastic style of construction, such as those of Nubt and Naqada (145-54). In Abadiyeh, a walled town was found similar to those towns depicted in the palettes; the hieroglyph "niwt" meaning city, also was found being used in this context and with the same meaning in Predynastic times! (149), (fig. 5).

A contrast between the occupations of Merimda and Maadi in Lower Egypt and those of Hierakonpolis and Badari in Upper Egypt was that in the first two sites the prehistoric population was concentrated in large, deep sites that had been occupied for long periods of time. Instead, the last two sites were spread out and shallow resulting in structural remains often not being preserved. This explanation accounts for the fact that settlements in areas of Upper Egypt were difficult to assess in terms of population density and agricultural potential. Although these sites were thought to be poor and without much agricultural capacity, they were proven by Butzer to have been the richest areas in southern Egypt which supported the largest populations. These factors may account for the reasons why the largest and most complex centers in Egypt were situated in the South. The evidence for this assertion is that Guy Brunton's excavations at Hierakonpolis found at least six pottery kilns where pottery was being fired after modeling and which attested for "the internal complexity and industrial-architectural sophistication of large Predynastic centers as Hierakonpolis" (Hoffman, 1979:148-150). Brunton also uncovered at Hierakonpolis a quantity of objects that he couldn't explain their purpose or use but which fit the description of tokens given by Schmandt-Besserat (fig. 9). See Appendix 1-6.

Late 1990, Hermann Junker excavated Merimda Beni Salama, a town situated thirty-seven miles northwest of Cairo, and he provided information about occupation, burial style, and female and child mortality which were tied to the farming practices. This community was much like that of the Qadan sites: people were interred within the settlements and their graves were almost never accompanied by offerings. A good stratigraphy at Merimda showed a continued occupation from 6000-4880 B.C. Junker reported in his notes the importance of this town and how well organized it was since the houses

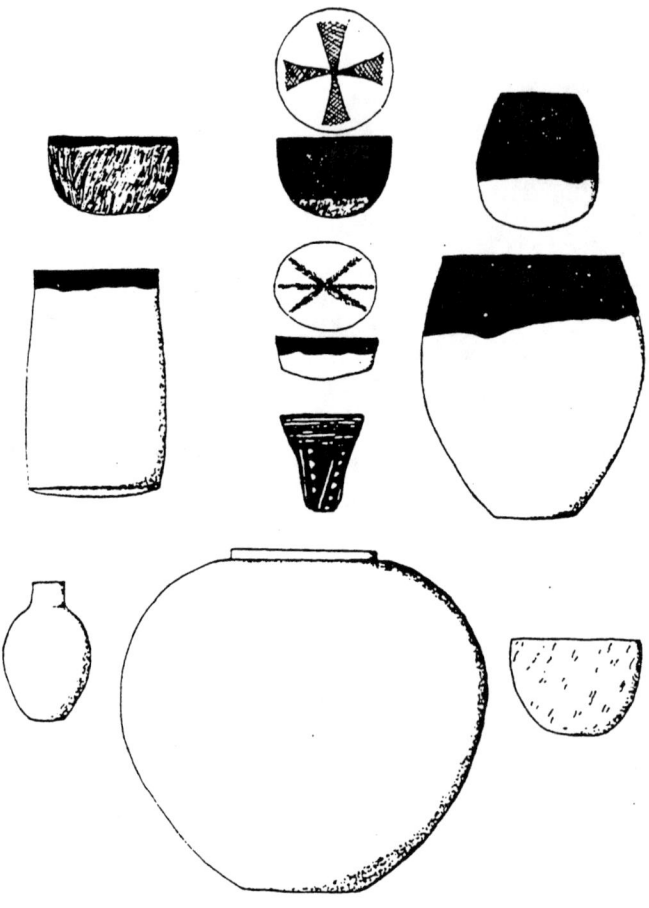

Assorted Badarian pottery, ca. 5500–4000 B.C.

Printed "Niwt" Sign from Abadiyah
(Drawings by Alicia Meza)

presented "living floors" with surrounding fences and granaries in a life style recalling the Mediterranean cultures of Palestine, Cyprus, and Mesopotamia (176) (Hoffman 169-176).

The site of Abydos was excavated by T. Eric Peet, 1914, who, despite the small area excavated, found settlements arranged in concentric circles and grain-parching kilns. The evidence of hamlets of a specialized community showed the use of copper tools to work exotic stones, such as carnelian, agate, quartz crystal, and diorite. Among the objects recovered, Peet also found impressed clay labels. These pattern dates to the start of the Predynastic at about 5000-3300 B.C. (150-54).

Gertrude Caton-Thompson, 1928, and Elinor Gardner excavated Fayum demonstrating that Fayum B had preceded Fayum A, which was an agricultural society since grain in silos dating from 5000 B.C. was found there. Lots of polished pottery, pigments, palettes, and stone bowls also were recovered at this site. Fayum B existence commenced at about 6000 B.C. until 4000 B.C., when Fayum A began. This culture was compared to Merimda and presents a sharp contrast in pottery style to the cultures of Upper Egypt. Fayum A also was linked to the Kharga culture in the western Oasis that subsequently was linked to the Merimda and Mediterranean cultures (Hoffman 1979:182-185). Perhaps the sea shells found at these sites were being used as money to exchange goods following a tradition from other Mediterranean peoples.

At El Omari, Fernand Debono, 1943, excavated a site near Helwan at Gebel El Tura at about 4000 B.C. Debono found at El Omari individual reed-fenced houses which seem to have been inhabited by nuclear families. The strata revealed occupations of Omari A, Omari B, and Omari C; Omari A had been successor to Merimda and Fayum A of the fourth millennium B.C. which were more connected to the valley cultures (191-99). The strata of Omari C was archaic and indicated connections to early Dynastic times; small stones were found in graves which may have been used as tokens.

The town of Maadi was by far one of the most important communities and a very cosmopolitan one. It was situated 10 km from Omari near Wadi El Tih, from where it dominated the trade to the Mediterranean sea and to the Indus Valley during 3600-3000 B.C. The houses were built underground in the style of houses found at the site of Bersheeba in southern Palestine. The Maadian houses had rooms for storage where there were lots of vessels made of different stones that seem to have been used for exchange. Carnelian beads, scoops, and small pots also were found at this important center. Kantor links this culture to the desert nomads through whom Maadi may have achieved exchange with other regions from afar. The copper industry in Maadi also was linked to trade since this center had a large industry using the ore from the desert, allowing Maadi to export its finished products to other areas as part of a long-range trade connection (Hoffman 1979:200-214).

At about 3600 B.C. there was a change in burial tradition in Lower Egypt, which adopted customs from Upper Egypt, a manifestation of social changes and possible influence from foreign contacts. According to a depiction on labels, the nomad dwellers of the Red Sea area in the eastern desert were engaged in trade, perhaps the same long-range trade to Mesopotamia which they were probably controlling the copper trade. These nomads also may have been the same middlemen who were engaged in trade from Egypt to India. This route over the eastern hills to the Red Sea can be inferred from a scene depicted on an ivory label in which King Den from the First Dynasty is seen smiting an enemy. The Easterner appears to be coming out of the mountains, and he has a standard surmounted on a straight-hulled boat which was classified by Frankfort as a Mesopotamian ship. Hoffman interprets this scene rather as two Egyptian men fighting for control over access to the Nile. Nevertheless, the scene involves desert dwellers.

At Saqqara, Emery, 1939, discovered in tomb 3035 inlaid alabaster disks! At Helwan, south of present day Cairo, Saad unearthed 10,258 tombs where he found the already famous "gaming pieces," cylinder seals, and ivory labels. Other finds of pot-marks, labels, and plaques were unearthed by Petrie at Abydos and by Green and Quibell at Hierakonpolis, where the ivories found by Petrie were linked to Gerzean times, 3600 B.C. These ivories and the "gaming pieces" are part of the collection of the Museum of the University College, London.

Hoffman, (1982) in explaining different features found at Kom El Ahmar, such as culinary, domestic, and miscellaneous features, reports that in storage pits there were small lumps of burnt clay listed in his report with an interrogation mark on the side, meaning Hoffman did not know what these clay lumps were used for. (Similar to fig. 6)

On the first two seasons at Hierakonpolis (1972), W.A. Fairsevis reports that two groups of Predynastic settlements were uncovered there. One settlement was where the main wadi emerges from the area of erosion and deposition; the other settlements were closer to the cultivation area on either side of the mouth of the great wadi. On phase C was the last major occupation from which hearths and traces of charcoal and ash were unearthed along with "baked clay objects in the shape of dog's biscuits of unknown function." The dating of this find is about 3800-3600 B.C.! A village of this phase C may have consisted of nucleated households gathered about some public structure which was represented by a stone pile, outside of which were individual households in relative isolation along the cultivated land.

Kom El Ahmar's building IV produced interesting features: in a small compartment of the large circle IV5 there were a group of ostrich egg-shaped stones of "unknown purposes." Also there were two river pebbles with grooves punctured with small scattered holes, that suggest a cord

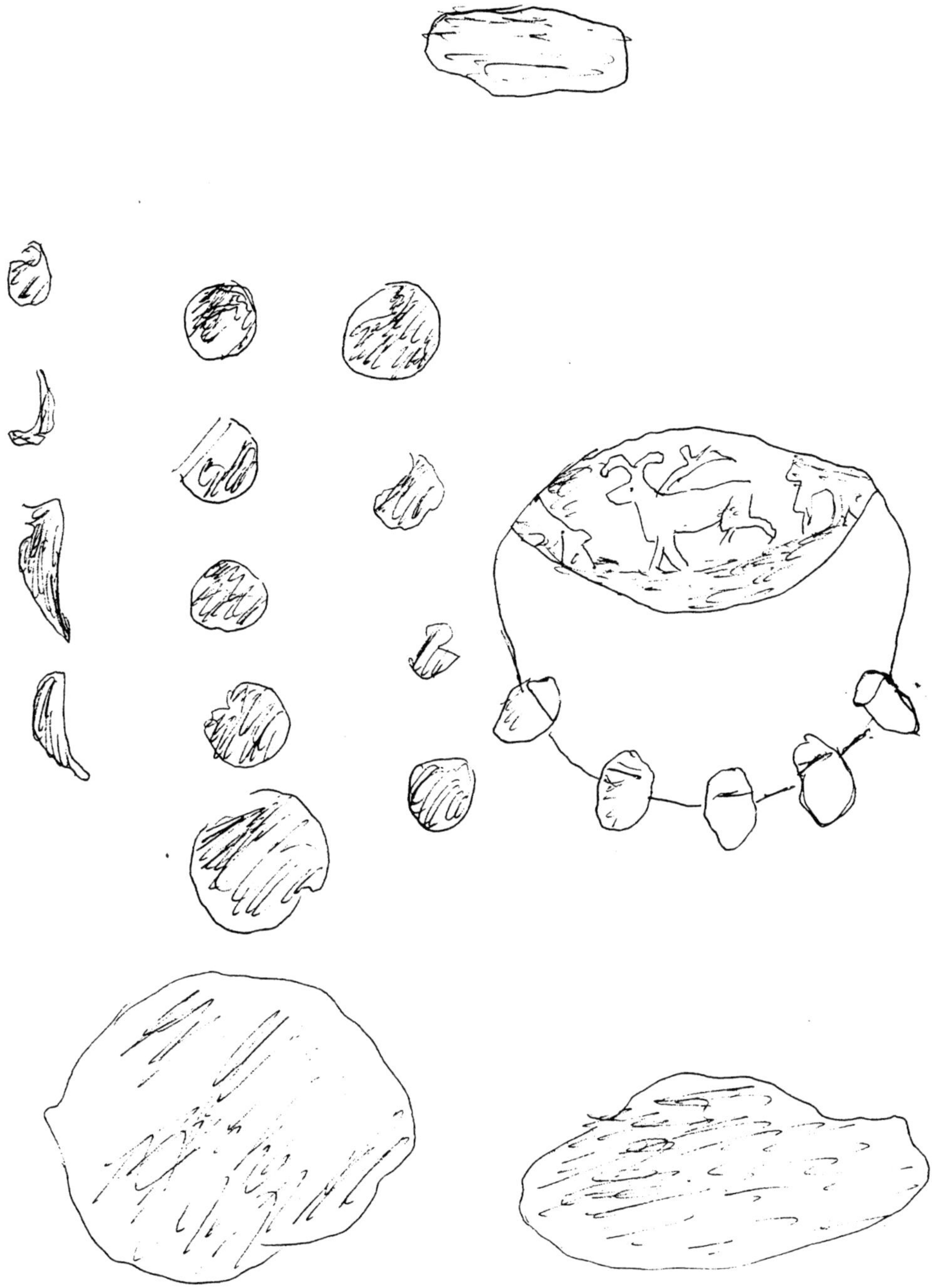

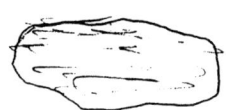

Bullae and Tokens from Mesopotamia
(Drawings by Alicia Meza)

passed through them (Fairsevis, 1978). These objects were found at the "junk deposit" behind the niched gate at the Hierakonpolis temple.

A chart in the appendix is showing the correlation of each token's shape and type from both Schmandt-Besserat's and Fairsevis' "gaming pieces" and "unknown objects" from the "junk deposit." Some of these objects are painted and perforated and, in one instance, there is an envelope among them. Some impressed tablets also were found at the "junk deposit"; one of the sherds had the "niwt" sign painted on it. Along with these tokens and envelopes, a cluster of six clay sealings also were found in a corner of the room. It seems this room was a service area of the temple; a parallel with the description made by Schmandt-Besserat of the context in which tokens were discarded in Mesopotamia: near the temples' service deposits.

Predynastic Dating and Social Complexity

J.F. Harlan proposes a new reorganization of the dates for the Predynastic periods. The periods are divided in three phases: Badarian, Early Predynastic Amratian or Naqada I and the Late Predynastic Gerzean or Naqada II. The Late Predynastic is followed by the Protodynastic or Naqada III. The absolute chronology of those periods have been disputed. For instance, according to Butzer, the Badarian period dates from 5200-4600 B.C. and the Amratian from 4600-3050 B.C. This chronology is based on C14 and thermoluminescence dating. For Butzer, Naqada I and Naqada II are a single Late Predynastic culture. Caton-Thompson, using luminescence, obtained 5580-4360 B.C. for the Badarian period. Trigger, using C14 and luminescence, obtained 4400 B.C. for the Badarian period and 4000-3500 B.C. for the Amratian. The Gerzean was subdivided into Early and Late, which is the last of the Predynastic periods at 3500-3100 B.C. Hoffman agreed with this division, with the exception that the Badarian began at 5000 B.C.15

Several scholars have attempted to account for the causes of social development in the Nile Valley. For instance, Payne from the Ashmolean Museum did a study on the conflicts between Hierakonpolis and its adjacent areas. Emery and Petrie linked the production of surpluses which sustained population growth as attested during Gerzean times, to the development of social complexity. There also were relationships made between burial customs and social complexity, warfare, and monumental construction. Finds, such as the painted tomb at Hierakonpolis from the Gerzean period which employed eastern motifs, imported goods such as timber from Lebanon found at Abydos, obsidian, Mediterranean sea shells, and vases from Palestine, also were facts that, according to Hoffman, could all be related to exchange systems related to social relationships and the exchange of marriage alliances; a way to acquire these alliances was by exchanging wealth.

That these marriage alliances were part of the exchange system was a fact that later became tradition continued during Dynastic times. Early evidence of this type of marriage alliance is portrayed in the macehead from Hierakonpolis where the "Narmer wedding" to a northern Egyptian princess is supposedly depicted (Hoffman 1979:322, 340). The development of social complexity also has been linked to long-range trade and marriage alliance exchange, which may have incentivated production and full-time craft specialists. Although there was population growth during Gerzean times which could be used in relation to warfare, according to Carneiro's circumscription theory, Butzer's studies reveal that land scarcity was not a problem in Predynastic Egypt (Butzer, 1976:101-103).

Harlan uses ceramic analysis to explain sociological phenomena at Hierakonpolis by predicting on several assumptions: patterns of archaeological remains reflect a pattern of prehistorical behavior; variability in distribution of ceramic remains at a site or between contemporaneous sites results from specific activities or social groups; and technique of manufacturing pottery is learned and passed on to the next generation.

Harlan mentions how specialist production was identified in early states and linked to local exchange and centralization in the Susiana Plains during the Early and Middle Uruk periods, according to Johnson (1973:157-166), who indicates that specialization is reflected in increasing standardization and decreasing variability between contemporaneous sites and centralization or workshop.[16] Specialization in ceramic production is discernible in the centralization of kilns and ceramic workshops at some localities at Hierakonpolis, such as locality 33. Centralized pottery production may have produced a surplus that may have been stimulated by trade. Some wares at Hierakonpolis were similar to those of Naqada and the Abydos regions. These pots were probably imported since the material available in the Hierakonpolis area is different. This also is suggested by the impressive quantity of potsherds.

Regional Analysis in Mesopotamia and in Egypt

According to Johnson (1977) and the Central Place Function Theory, the exchange networks on the Susiana Plains during the fourth millennium B.C. presented evidence for contacts with outside regions. The centers for ceramic production and distribution were the indicators of monopolization in ceramic production, and these specific centers were directly connected to the central place. These events can be paralleled with those occurring in Egypt because the Nile Valley area had outside contacts during the Predynastic period that were probably part of the same exchange network with Mesopotamia. The ceramic production and distribution from the diverse Predynastic centers in Egypt were probably orchestrated in a similar way than those in Mesopotamia according to their importance and social complexity.

The evidence coming from Kathryn Bard's excavations with Boston University is from the sites located near Nag Hammadi (1989). At this site, a fragment of a mud sealing was found which was created by impressing a mud lump over three loops of string tied around a jar. This type of sealing suggests an exchange of valuable goods in a regional or long-distance exchange network that correlates with the grave goods excavated by Petrie (1896), who uncovered over two thousand graves on the northern and southern towns, and by Hassan, who found a seal with an inscribed hieroglyph for the word "gold," a very important commodity at this site. Naqada was engaged in trade along with Hierakonpolis, Abydos, and Maadi, where the copper trade was intensive because this site was near the mines at Gebel Ataqa and the Sinai. Proof for all this traffic was the Palestinian pottery and the raw materials found at Maadi, such as obsidian, lapis lazuli, bitumen, and resins, which were all status goods that had to be traded in since Egypt did not have all these materials available in the Valley area (Lucas, 1962). However, Egypt was able to trade these exotic commodities because the Nile Valley did not lack any subsistence goods and was rich in other types of raw materials, such as alabaster, marble, basalt, and gold.

According to Stevenson Smith (1992:235-46), the growth of trade in west Africa was responsible for social stratification since this growth in trade was promoted by the movement of peoples after the fifth millennium B.C. with the desiccation of the Western desert and the relocation of pastoralists and agriculturists into the Valley. This expansion of peoples and trade among the growing towns provoked conflicts for the trade routes and the access to the resources which, consequently, led to militarism and leadership. The evidence for these conflicts among towns was in the construction of those two-meter-thick walls, such as the mud-brick enclosure at the southern town in Naqada and the model of a walled town found by Petrie (1901) at Diaspolis Parva.

These speculations may be supported by Carneiro's Circumscription Theory also mentioned before by Harlan and which could be supported by the geographic evidence of Hierakonpolis, from where people may have expanded north to increase their agricultural holdings.

In this article about regional analysis in archaeology, Johnson indicated that direct interaction data is available to archaeologists involving distribution of goods for which location of production is known; the most common selected alternative to identify interaction has been post-marital residence.[17] Differences in distances between sites and source of material may result in different plots, from linear to flat, which according to Renfew would be an indication of a shift in size of interacting populations from general populations near source areas to increasingly specific subpopulations away from source areas.[18]

Johnson points out "increase in activity coordination among population units develops specialization and leadership to reduce costs of information transfer involved in coordination," and "if higher status individuals tend to be spatially localized within a settlement system and participate differently in long-range trade, the organization for the production of items for export, the concentration of craftsmen for the production of status-related items from imported and local material, and related activities may lead to further increase in functional size differentiation within the system." These processes may contribute to different distribution of functional sizes in a settlement system leading to hierarchical systems based on the effectiveness of coordination of the system. The increase in vertical complexity will favor the creation of different centers to minimize movement and costs. Functional size for unit of population decreases as population size increases, according to Zipf. Also a linear rank size distribution is produced by a high degree of integration among cities in economically developed countries. A deviation from the linear rank-size distribution, such as a primate distribution or concave plot, indicates large settlements are larger than expected and the small settlements are smaller than expected. Instead, a convex plot may indicate large settlements are smaller than expected and small settlements are larger than expected. Variability in rank-size distribution ranges from primate to linear to convex, which is the situation when size distribution of a settlement system approaches the discontinuous hierarchy posited by central place theory, at least in cases with multiple highest order central places. A convex rank-size distribution should indicate the possibility that relatively autonomous settlement systems are being combined in the analysis. Instead, concave rank-size distributions appear to be related to the political administration of an economy and the minimation of competition. Such studies have been applied by Johnson to the analysis of the development of the alluvial plain in southwestern Iran during the Terminal Susa A period, Early Uruk, Middle Uruk, and Late Uruk periods. The utility of this analysis is obviously important to infer information about long-term regional scale settlement pattern and about the interaction among cities, which gives information about social development and pristine state formation in the area. A similar study will be attempted in this paper to test social development and state formation throughout the Nile Valley area.

Chapter Six

Regional Archaeological Analysis

Before analyzing the rank-size distribution on Predynastic Egyptian settlements, to be able to compare this data with Johnson's on Mesopotamia it is worthwhile to examine some useful concepts on the development of decision-making organizations: how these decision-making hierarchies essentially allow the coordination of a large number of activities and/or the integration of a larger number of organizational units that would not be possible in the absence of such hierarchies (Johnson 1982); and how this development has as its end product the growth of social complexity and settlement size and, subsequently, pristine state formation.

According to Johnson, there are two kinds of basic processes by which decision-making organization increases in complexity: horizontal and vertical specialization. The first type is when the decision-making units increase at a given level of the organization; the second type is when the increase is made on the number of hierarchic-arranged levels of such organization. Johnson states that according to Regulation Theory, given two independent sets, variety in one set can be reduced only by increasing variety in the other set. For instance, an integrative mechanism is lacking within an organization to achieve integration of ideas or activities when there is a variety of decisions in this organization the only way to reduce this variety is to develop such integrative mechanism. Furthermore, independent increase in the variety of decisions required for the integration of a system which already is regulated by a specialized decision-making organization can only be reduced by increasing the variety of decisions made by that organization. The model for the development of decision-making organizations involves the relationship between the increase in differences of information sources integrated and the workload required to achieve that integration in the absence of a vertical specialized control mechanism. The number of one-to-one relationships among activities or other units which constitute effective information channels linking these units. Johnson observes that this load may be decreased by the development of a specialized vertical control mechanism. Workload in information transfer is reduced with vertical specialization and when more information sources are integrated, reducing the information channels used to achieve integration. Increase in vertical specialization and sources integrated decreases workload, but this rate decreases rapidly as there is an increasing pressure for division of labor (horizontal specialization) within a single unit of the vertical control mechanism. Administrative advantage decreases as horizontal specialization continues and such diminishing returns constitute an effective selection pressure for second-order vertical specialization, which becomes efficient when six units are integrated: six horizontal units of a first order vertical mechanism. Then the efficient development of a decision-making organization is extended to a third-order vertical specialization; the decrease of workload is the result of vertical and horizontal specialization of the control-mechanism complexity. Any deviation from a maximizing assumption involves marked increases in workload required for source information. Moreover, Johnson continues, if workload is directly related to effective costs, the increasing costs of deviation from efficiency in system integration may be related to an increased probability of system failure. Social processes facilitate and inhibit the cost-benefit optimization in the organization of societal levels should provide one source of explanation for the continued development or breakdown and failure of social systems.

Vertical specialization in administrative organization reduces workload in channel monitoring (information transfer). Instead, horizontal specialization reduces workload involved in explicit source integration which involves decision making. The workload reduction involves information processing; efficient increase in administrative complexity is associated with effective step function in administrative efficiency. Johnson observes that suppression of vertical and/or horizontal specialization in administrative organization produces a marked increase in workloads and costs involved in system integration. Suppression of first-order vertical specialization involves increments in information transfers and processing costs. Therefore, at the societal level the selective pressure for vertical specialization in decision-making organization also selects for the development of ascribed status that regularizes inheritance rules (ranking systems). Also, decision making involves the recruiting and training of personnel and the maintenance of organization continuity. Moreover, decision implementation requires the population acquiesce to carry out operational aspects of decisions made by vertically specialized personnel: the modification of behavior of another unit or individual by one individual or organizational unit. If differences in social status are positively related to differences in influence, then incorporating individuals with differentially higher status in a decision-making hierarchy should increase the probability of decision implementation. With the development and implementation of regular-status inheritance rules, the problems of recruitment, training, and continuity may be reduced by designating individuals to occupy decision-making positions. These individuals would be trained for these activities during childhood. Also according to Johnson, the problem of organizational continuity may be thus solved: a difference in the type of social organization Sahlins makes between "big man" societies, which lack continuity, recruiting, and training, and chiefdom societies which have an increased potential for such activities. The development of ranking systems may be associated with the increment in the number of differences of information sources integrated on a societal level. Johnson mentions Fried's proposed processes to increment the development of ranking systems, such as maintaining connections between parent settlements and those that have budded off; diversifying the consuming sector of the economy by maintaining regular trade relations with communities exploiting different resources; organizing labor forces for better handling of food-supply and irrigation tasks; absorbing new settlers in the already established settlements; and formalizing trans-settlement sodalities.

To take these processes into account is important when looking at the emergence of prehistorical cities in the ancient Egyptian countryside. By budding off, these settlements covered all the Nile Valley area, linking the Delta to Nubia, in a network of centers for ceramic production and social and religious activities that were responsible for the development of an homogeneous Egyptian cultural identity, which was consolidated later with the unification. Not only these processes mentioned by Johnson and proposed by Fried were probably responsible for the development of the Egyptian settlement system. These processes also were responsible for the development of an intraregional trade network that linked Egypt to Mesopotamia, and which also probably involved a mating network, well-known and abundantly recorded during the Dynastic era.

The rapid increase in the number of management hierarchies within these Egyptian centers were triggered by forces operating from within those organizational units or settlements. Johnson mentions the studies made by Udy that predict the number of levels of management hierarchy appropriate for coordination of a given number of activities. The maximum numbers of items which an individual can give simultaneous attention, and, therefore, the maximum numbers of activities an administrator can effectively coordinate, ranges between three and seven with a mode of five. In activity coordination this number is probably four. Any deviation from this efficiency consideration would result in marked increase of workload, taxing individuals and unit capacities. Systems in which a highest-order control unit attempts to integrate a number of subordinates in excess of six or seven individuals is under considerable pressure for horizontal specialization of that highest-order unit. On the societal level this fact should be reflected in increasing administrative costs and in the attempts by the population of the society to induce such specialization. Also Johnson indicates that the integration of a large number of subordinate units by a single-unit, highest-order vertical control mechanism may indicate a low level of integration. The degree of this integration among settlements can be tested by plotting the settlements in a ranking-size distribution. Furthermore, the volume of trade involved in the local intraregional exchange also can be calculated in basis to the surplus extracted from food production and its consumption. Johnson, in his article "Dynamics of Southwestern Prehistory" (1989), explains that elites were built on surpluses. He calculates that 5 ha of agricultural land per capita would have been an estimate of the subsistence requirement in Prehistoric southwestern Iran. Prehistoric villages could cultivate about 2 ha of land per capita, and because 1.5 ha per capita would be destined to elite consumption, 75 percent of the agricultural product could be diverted to public use without endangering the producing population. These figures were the approximate surplus extracted by the population of southwestern Iran during the fourth millennium B.C. In addition, food surplus from the center's populations and substantial center and rural labor during nonagricultural seasons also may be considered to calculate the volume of produce used in consumption, ritual, and trade.

Besides learning about the degree of integration among settlements, the size-frequency distribution of settlements in a settlement system can be used to signal the operation of a variety of potential boundary phenomena (Johnson, 1977). This strategy is based on rank-size rule in geography which relies on the notion that settlement systems contain few large centers and a greater proportion of increasingly smaller settlements. The plot of these settlements gives a negative skew in the direction of the smaller settlements. This plotting consists of a descending array of settlements by their size against settlement rank in that descending array of sizes. The rank-size rule consists of an empirical observation: rank-size distribution from many different settlement systems of a rank "r" in the descending array of settlement sizes has a size equal to $1/r$ of the size of the largest settlement in the system. For instance, the second settlement would be one-half of the first or largest settlement, the third, one-third, and so on. When the tenth settlement is one-tenth the size of the largest settlement and is plotted on a double logarithmic scale, the resulting curve is a straight line with a slope of -1. Zipf has suggested that a linear rank-size distribution is produced by a high degree of interaction in an economically developed country, although some countries do not produce such straight-line curves.

Johnson explains that his work also has attempted to solve the apparent conflict between the rank-size rule and central place theory. The former posits continuous settlement size distributions; the latter posits discontinuos distributions containing discrete levels of settlement-size hierarchy. The discontinuity of local size distributions may appear to be continuous if local areas are pooled together, such as when the curve is deviated in a convex line. Convexity results in cases when the largest settlement in the system is smaller than predicted. Convexity also is attributed to the pooling of independent or relatively independent settlement systems and to the presence of significant interactional boundaries within the area under analysis. The other basic deviation from rank-size linearity is when the plot is primate or concave, indicating the largest settlement is larger than expected. The factors responsible for this kind of plotting are various, such as the dominance of a primate center to the high availability of low-cost labor and when economic competition among settlements is politically minimized. The system also may be connected to an outside system, such as the case of colonial empires in which a colonial capital would be more closely articulated with the rest of the empire than would other colonial settlements.

According to Johnson, in highly integrated systems the size of a given settlement is dependent upon (a conditional function of) the sizes of other settlements in the system. The settlements are linked by a variety of social, economic, and political processes which affect settlement sizes. If settlement-system integration is defined in terms of statistical interdependence of settlement sizes, determination of settlement sizes should follow the rule of conditional probabilities and be a multiplicative function. Therefore, a highly integrated system would approach a normal-log plot. Meanwhile, a convex distribution would indicate a low integrated system which, by becoming increasingly integrated, its rank-size distribution should become less convex and increasingly log-normal. Johnson presents the data obtained from the Susiana Plains of southwestern Iran during the Terminal Susa A to Middle Uruk (3800-3400 B.C.). The plain at 3800 B.C. was occupied by four enclaves of settlements representing remnant population from a breakup of a larger society in the previous period. The rank-size plot at this time is very convex. After new settlements were founded in the area and the western portion of the plain was coming under the administrative control of elites located at two emerging centers, of which Susa was the dominant, the plot was still convex but markedly less than earlier.

As the elites were able to extract surpluses from the agricultural produce and labor, rural populations were incorporated into the administration of center control. Sealed shipments of commodities were being moved in increasing volume between centers and rural areas, and the increasing workload had been met by both vertical and horizontal expansion of the administrative system. At this time, 3400 B.C., Susa had a size of 25 ha with an estimated population of around five thousand people dominating a three-level administrative hierarchy with a total population of about twenty-one thousand people. The rank-size distribution reflecting the increase in system integration was very nearly log-normal.

As stated before by Johnson, a convex distribution can be created by either pooling separate systems or by partitioning an individual system. A convexity exhibited in peripheral areas of larger systems is related to the organization of a dendritic system. Dendritic systems normally exhibit regional primacy and decrease in settlement functional size with increasing distance from the system primate center through which lower-level settlements are integrated. Horizontal interaction among lower-level settlements at the same level of hierarchy is weak. Material, personnel, and information flows are primarily vertical between the system primate center and lower order centers. Since additive process produces consistently hyper-convex distributions and multiplicative processes very rapidly generates nearly lognormal distributions, the determinants of lower-order settlement sizes are thus probably largely additive and their low level of horizontal integration should generate rank-size convexity. Johnson mentions the case presented by Paynter in which peripheries of dendritic systems show convex distributions. Their cores, meanwhile, should exhibit primate distributions: a "primo-convex" plot. Such is the case, presented by Johnson, in the Warka area of southern Mesopotamia between 3600-3200 B.C. This area presented at the beginning of this time period a very primate distribution that later became increasingly log-normal.

At 3600 B.C. the Warka area was occupied by a dendritic system with a four-level settlement hierarchy centered on the site of Warka itself. Warka provided an administrative integration for the four enclaves of settlement which apparently had little interaction among themselves. Enclave-center size was positively related to the sum of the sizes of associated settlements within each enclave, and the individual sizes of enclave centers and larger villages were inversely related to distance from the system primate center at Warka. The system having a low integration interaction at the horizontal-settlement level and strongly developed vertical administration from Warka exhibited a primo-convex distribution.

By 3200 b.c a considerable change in settlement-system spatial distribution within the Warka area showed a lattice with five large centers and associated settlements. The system also showed small specialized administrative sites marking the boundaries of the immediate hinterlands of adjacent centers. Although Warka was still the largest site, the system now exhibited a nearly log-normal settlement rank-size distribution. Archaeological material characteristic of Warka found beyond its immediate hinterland indicates the system was probably connected with an other larger system or that further settlements dependent on Warka were articulated with it. Johnson concludes that, perhaps, a combination of systems internal and external or boundary phenomena were responsible for such rank-size distribution.

Plotting the Predynastic Egyptian settlements in a rank-size distribution presents the problem of using accurate archaeological data throughout the fourth millennium B.C. An approximate estimate in settlement size also using discriminating criteria for rank-size finally produces two types of plots that could be interpreted as "early" data and a "later" or more developed type of settlement rank-size distribution.

The problem with Egyptian archaeology is that very seldom field reports present accurate site measurements. Those that do so present the further problem that the stratification of several time-period occupations within the same area, combined with the search for sekhba or fertilizing material for cultivation done by the locals, produce a kind of "nightmarish" conclusive data to use for settlement rank-size distribution analysis during different periods of the fourth millennium B.C.

Nevertheless, persistence and a time-consuming search produced two kinds of rank-size distribution. In the first Hierakonpolis or the Nekhben area, which would be the largest settlement within the Hierakonpolitan area, thirteen settlements of unknown individual size total an amount of 2,000 ha, appears to have been an 82-hectare site (Hierakonpolis). The other sites, Naqada which was the rival center of Hierakonpolis, also an enclave of nine settlements of probably a total of 360 ha, but with the site of Nubt as the largest settlement with 40 ha. Omari in the Maadi region had 38 ha. Abydos, which later became an important center, had 27 ha. This site also presents the problem of having been used as a cemetery and being near the Naqada area. It is unclear whether it was part habitational or totally a burial place. Buto was the rival and counterpart center of Hierakonpolis in the Delta. It also was an important center in this area, with a continuous habitation which had a size of about 22 ha; Merimda Beni Salama in the western Delta apex had 16 ha; Maadi had 15 ha; Tell el Awad near Buto had 6 ha; El Kab, the twin city of Hierkonpolis on the other bank of the Nile, presented at this time about 4 ha; Ezbet el Tell, also near Buto, had 2 ha; and the region near Badari presented Abadiyah with 2 ha. This region had several settlements that amounted to about 55 ha total.

The resulting plot of this settlement system rank-size distribution is a convex line that approaches the log-normal line and later falls in its tail (fig. 7). Perhaps at this time settlements were not well integrated in a system, but they, nevertheless, had trade and cultural exchange with each other. Grouping the sites by regions, such as the Buto region and the Hierakonpolis region, produced twice about the same results using about the same data (fig. 8-9). Hierakonpolis was very convex, dropping then nearly the log-normal line. Buto, instead, curiously gives twice a primate distribution. I interpret these two different distributions as being two independent systems. Hierakonpolis in the South and Buto in the North in the Delta heart near the Sinai region. It is interesting to see that the primate distribution presented by Buto may indicate a connection with an outside system in Palestine, Mesopotamia, or the Hierakonpolitan region in the South. The convex distribution this last region presented instead may indicate that, although intrasettlement integration was weak, the plot approaches closely then the log-normal line.

Another rank-size distribution I have made, just to be on the safe side, was using measurements of whole enclaves as a sole settlement. In this way

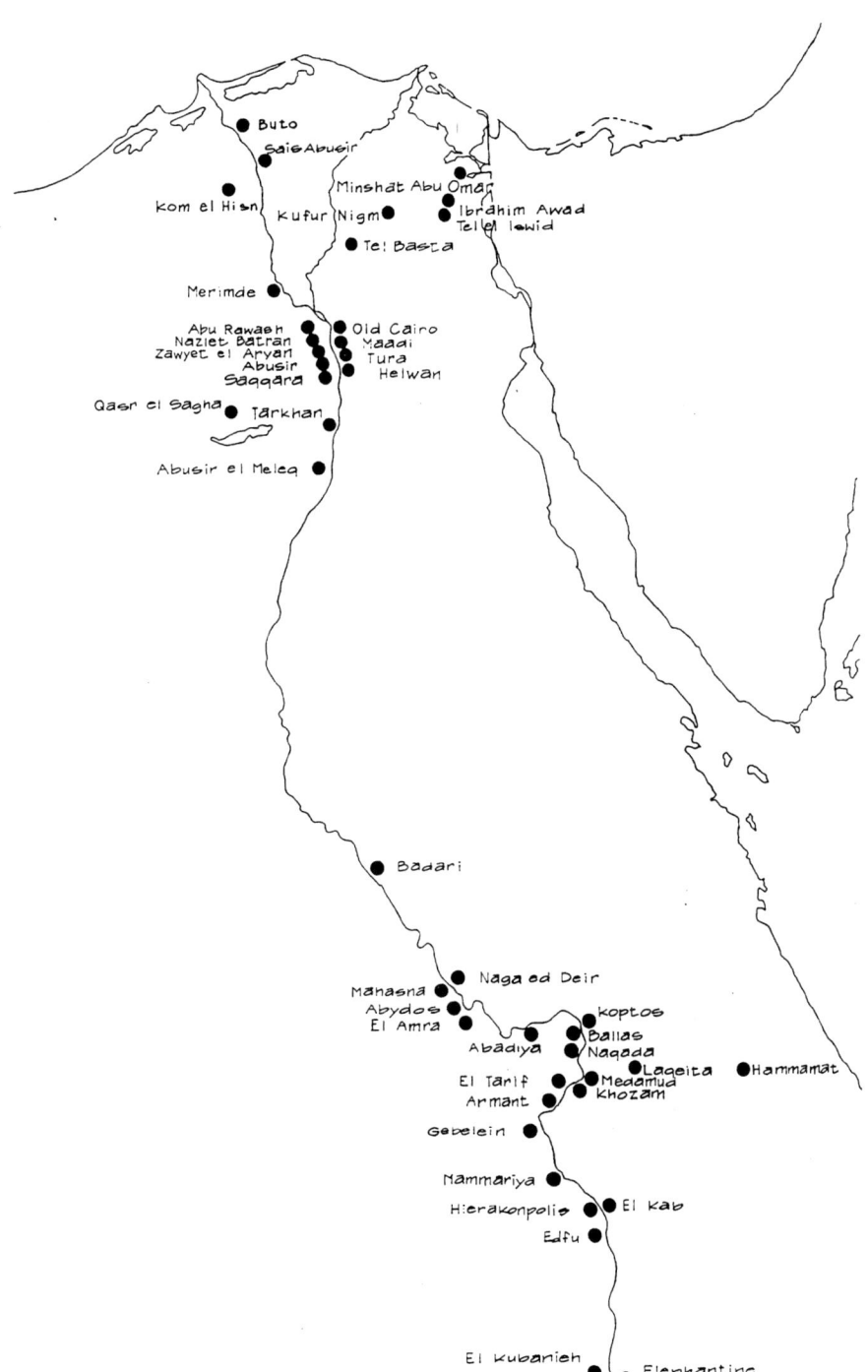

I had a system which was the whole area from the Delta to Hierakonpolis (fig. 10). Twice the distribution becomes convex, although the first time is primate and then convex; the second time I plotted it was convex log-normal then convex but near the log-normal distribution. The pooling of systems, according to Johnson, may produce this kind of distribution and the Egyptian towns obliged.

Finally, the last plot of settlement-size distribution (fig. 11) with the best data I could find gave me a size of 154 ha for Hierakonpolis; Naqada, 50 ha; Abydos, 40 ha; Omari, 38 ha; Badari, 24 ha; Buto, still 22 ha; Fayum, 20 ha, an approximation really; el Kab, 20 ha; Maadi, 18 ha; Merimda, 16 ha; Tell el Awad, still 6 ha; Ezbet Tell, 5 ha; Abadyah, 1.5 ha; and Semainah, 1 ha.

The distribution obtained is primate and then rapidly approached the log-normal, dwindling a little to primate but returning to log-normal. The conclusion is that the total system may have been primate when pooled or connected to an outside system, or, simply, it may have been growing dendritic with centers becoming larger with a centralized ceramic production. The centralized ceramic production connected to the main center Hierakonpolis, which later became its first capital, is Harlan's theory. Nevertheless, a histogram (fig. 12) indicates a four-hierarchy settlement system was in operation at this time. Rank-size indexes and ceramic analyses may produce more information.

Chapter Seven

Archaeological Reports and Publications

Emery did extensive work at Saqqara and other Predynastic sites in Egypt. The Predynastic material he uncovered presented an obvious connection with Mesopotamian art style (1961:30-40, 165-89). This influence was imprinted in the representation of animals with entwined necks depicted on the Narmer palette (fig. 1) and in the birds standing in a row as shown on seals and decorations (fig. 8). This style association made by Emery also was corroborated by other scholars (Frankfort, 1948; Fischer, 1990; Baumgartel, 1947), who hinted that this distribution could have been a result of artisans traveling from on area to another, bringing with them their own styles and skills. This factor also could explain how some Egyptian pot-marks may have had a correspondence of design to the markings on Mesopotamian tokens (fig. 1-2 in the appendix).

Emery mentions a series of disks of stone, copper, wood, and ivory which, along with small stone marbles, "would appear to have been used as counters"; others found in trays at Saqqara "would appear to have been part of a game" (1961:48), (fig. 4). These disks seem similar in form and in design to the Mesopotamian tokens and disks described in Schmandt-Besserat's corpus. They have a diameter of four inches with a hole in the middle through which was a pointed stick of six inches long. The meaning of this stick is not clear, but the disks look exactly like perforated tokens.[19]

The commodities that may have reached Mesopotamia from Egypt may have been, as mentioned earlier, raw materials such as alabaster from the mines at Hat-nub in the Eastern desert behind Helwan, basalt extracted from the Fayum area, and diorite from the Eastern desert, Aswan, and Nubia. Breccia was mined at a site near Esna in Upper Egypt, and dolomite

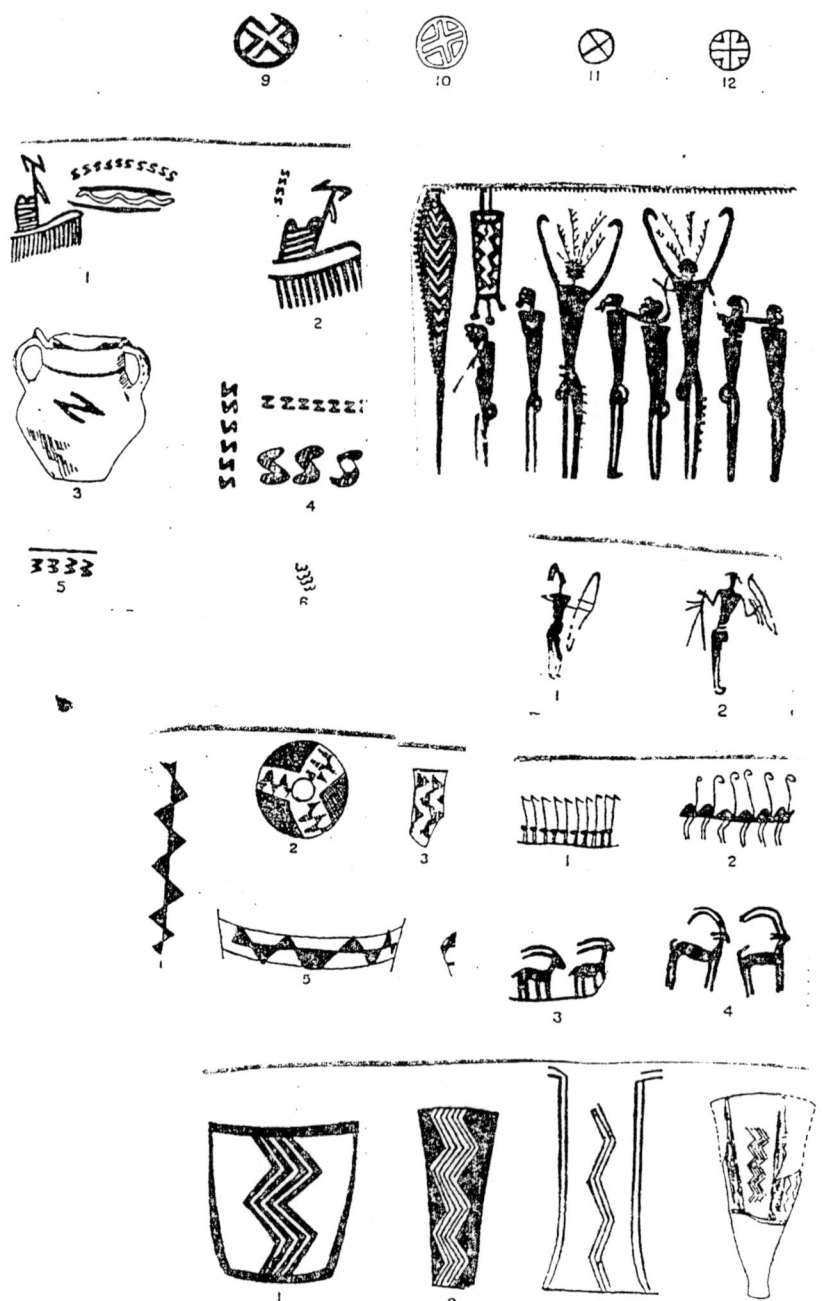

Wavy Lines, "Niwt" Sign and "Z" Sign
(Drawings by Alicia Meza)

was extracted in the Western Desert. Schist and volcanic ash were procured at Wadi Hammamat, and marble and porphyritic rock were extracted in the Red Sea coast area; purple porphyry was found in Gebel Dokhan in the Eastern Desert, and serpentine and rock crystal also were coming from the Eastern Desert. From Sinai other raw materials were extracted and exported, such as copper, malachite, and turquoise. The export of stone vessels and precious stones, such as agate, onyx, amethyst, carnelian, chalcedony, green feldspar, and garnet halmatite jasper made possible the acquisition of lapis lazuli (Lucas, 1962). The last stone was considered a sacred material by the Egyptians; lapis lazuli was cherished by their gods as related in the story of the "Shipwreck Sailor" of the Old Kingdom.

Mesopotamian Influence in Egyptian Predynastic Art

E.J. Baumgartel also has associated the art style of Predynastic Egypt with that of Mesopotamia. By examining the fragment of a large Hierakonpolis mace-head with an impressed rosette on it, Baumgartel made some important observations (1966:9-13). For instance, she indicates that this motif has been represented in several circumstances in Egyptian history, such as in the knife handles of King Senefru and in the slate palettes of King Narmer and King Scorpion (fig. 7).
Baumgartel explains that the rosette has been associated with the copulating snakes, a motif rare in Egyptian representation but common in Sumer where it represents fertility. In Sumer the rosette means fertility and belongs to the Great Goddess, also meaning good augury. Baumgartel also thinks the rosette may have been associated with the Egyptian goddess Sheshat with a parallel symbolism than in Mesopotamia, as it is depicted in the foundation ceremony of Hierkonpolis carved in the macehead.

The scorpion, on the other hand, depicted together with the rosette, was a symbol of motherhood in both Mesopotamia and Egypt. In Mesopotamia the scorpion is present under the marriage couch at the "sacred marriage" (fig. 9). In Egypt the scorpion goddess holds the feet of the god Amun in the marriage scene of Amun and the queen mother of Amenhotep III in the temple of Luxor; this scorpion has a life sign in each of its foremost claws. The scorpion also protected Isis when she was hiding with Horus in the marshes of the Delta. Dozens of scorpions were found at the main deposit at Hierakonpolis as ex-vota to the goddess. Just as the rosette, it became a goddess: the goddess Selket. From very early times during Naqada II they were represented on pottery in Egypt (fig. 7). In the Sumerian concept, the ear corn was a glyptic for the great goddess' male companion. In Egypt the ear corn may have represented Horus, who also was identified with Min the ithyphallic god of harvest. Horus may

The Scorpion Palette
(Drawing by Alicia Meza)

have been the counterpart of the scorpion and the rosette which stand for the goddess (fig. 7).

Another similitude Baumgartel attributes to Mesopotamian influence is in the slate palettes' depictions of sertpent-necked felines, such as those of the Narmer palette that has a counterpart in the stella of King Eannatum of Lagash (fig. 1), (1960:81-105). However, Ranke thinks this motif is of Libyan influence and that it is depicting the marshes in the Delta. Vandier also relates these places depicted in the palettes to the Delta, but he admits a Sumerian influence is seen in the two giraffes chewing palm leaves.

Palettes are among the objects found by Petrie. Some palettes are small, about 5 cm, and can fit the description for tokens. In a tomb, a necklace was found that had disk-shaped beads of steatite, carnelian, turquoise, and quartzite. Petrie had described some of the objects as "curios egg-shaped pot painted with cross-lined drawings"; another string of pierced natural flint "pebbles" and pierced shells which may have been Naqada II were found along with some lumps of malachite and one little cone covered with leather "which could have belonged to a game." Ivory tags also were found among these artifacts, some of them incised with diagonal lines. All these objects are at the Ashmolean Museum in Oxford.

There also is a Mesopotamian influence in mace-heads, which also depict the rosette, the symbol of Ishtar, and the scorpion, the symbol of fertility and motherhood (Baumgartel, 1960:154). The scorpion in Egyptian ichnography is the symbol for Selket, the goddess who causes the throats to breathe and who may have been connected to the goddess Hathor, this being the reason she became so important at Hierakonpolis.

A little mace-head of about 3 cm was found at Hierakonpolis by Quibell. It had engraved on it the classical Mesopotamian motif of lions biting dogs and dogs biting lions. The cult to the fertility goddess during Naqada I can be seen in the tombs from Naqada where she also is associated with Hathor in the depiction of her symbol, the cow horns, along with her male companion, who also is her son and lover and who also was venerated at this time. Her lover is depicted as "ka mut.ef" or the "bull of his mother," a title given to the kings of Egypt during dynastic times. The god Min, from Coptos is the strong bull, who later also was represented as an ithyphallic god, meaning fertility. According to Baumgartel's interpretation, perhaps the early kings who performed the fertility ritual were called "Nswt," also a title given to later Dynastic kings. This fertility symbol reflected the important position that later women were going to hold in Egyptian society.

In the production of pottery, Baumgartel (1955:102-3) indicates that the slow wheel may have come to Egypt during Naqada II, and this innovation may have played a part in the manufacture of spouted wares. Bell pot, which was Uruk stratum XII running to stratum IV, was classified by Petrie as wares "R" and "L," both of them common during Naqada II. The loop-handled pot was rare in Egypt, and Kantor relates this pottery to Palestine and Naqada I as Petrie had done. However, Baumgartel does not agree with this origin because the loop-handled pot also has been found at Susa and at Yorgan Tepe during the Uruk period. Baumgartel adds that the herringbone-incised pottery found by Caton-Thompson has parallels in Badari, Yorgan Tepe, Nuzi, Al Ubaid, and Niniveh; another type, which has the fingertips incised on the pot, has been found at Hammamieh, Naqada, Yorgan Tepe, and early Naqada II. For Baumgartel these Egyptian pottery types depend on the prototypes from early Uruk.

However, certain pottery types were reelated to Nubia. For instance, the black-incised pottery from Naqada I, such as the Tasian beaker, is related to the Pan Grave people and to the cultures from Nubia. The white-incised pottery was attributed to the Khartum Neolithic, according to Arkell. When Griffith excavated at Faras, he related the black-mouthed pottery found there to the Badarian pottery. All these relationships mean that, although Mesopotamian styles were being used, the Nubian cultures also were being blended into the Egyptian Predynastic culture.

According to Baumgartel, the similarities between Egypt and Mesopotamia were constricted to the similarities in art style between Susa I and Naqada I when both cultures shared similar geometric waving lines in their artistic representations (fig. 13), (1955: 49-12; 1960). Al Ubaid and Naqada styles both had triangles arranged in rows filled with paint, a motif common in Egypt, Mesopotamia, and Iran. Baumgartel indicates that patterning in these styles is created to convey a special meaning, such as the wavy line conveying liquids contained in the vessels so inscribed as, for instance, the three wavy lines that mean "water" in Phoenician and in ancient Egyptian. Falkenstein indicates that signs used in Uruk and in Naqada I pottery were prototypes of hieroglyphs; in this way two wavy lines for "water" were transformed in cuneiform Sumerian Akkadian "mw," water. In early Egyptian the lines were vertical instead of horizontal, a fact that proves the different origins for the interpretation and depiction of water. Later the lines also were written horizontally in Egypt.

Other motifs used in both Mesopotamian and Egyptian art styles were animals, such as goats, bulls, and sheep, which also were represented by the horns. The representational style of part of the body profile and part of the body front also were used and shared by Susa and Egypt, as it is seen in two vases depicting archers. A pond drawn with circles at the bottom of the vase has convergent wavy lines of water also depicted in vases from Badari, Susa, and Persepolis. A Badarian vase with the pond motif has four buffaloes with long horns grouped around the middle of the vase; a circle in the middle has a cross (1955:55-84). This circle with the cross is the ancient Egyptian hieroglyph for the word "niwt," or "town" (fig. 8). Baumgartel interprets this cross as the pond having four equal arms, a motif shared by Diaspolis Parva, Naqada, Susa, and Persepolis. This sign, "niwt," also is similar to another from the Uruk tablets and it is equated by Falkenstein with the Asyrian which means "to take," or "take possession." Two more pattern examples from Susa and Naqada show branch-like designs near the cross, which may have had the same symbolism in both places. The sequence dating for this type of design is, according to Brunton, Petrie's SD31 to 34, corresponds to the Naqada I period. The second pattern is the net pattern, which also occurs in Susa and Naqada I. The animal motif is used more in Egypt than in Mesopotamia, which uses more geometric designs. Egypt had more of a tendency to destroy the regularity of geometric patterns by adding water lines to the design (55). Baumgartel's conclusion is that, in this sense, the influence on Egyptian style is more from Iran than from Mesopotamia, which also drew from Iran.

Other imported designs used in Egypt were: the Red Sea boats from Naqada I, the row of long-neck birds, and the goats from Susa introduced to Egypt during Naqada II times; the "z" sign used in Egyptian pottery is also probably of Asiatic origin (fig. 8); the pentagram motif also is shared by Naqada, Diaspolis Parva, and Jemdat el Nasr; and the spiral motif is typical Egyptian, although one example comes from Iran (55-79). All these symbols used in Babylonia, Egypt, and Iran may have been understood by the potter who copied them since they convey meaning. Pictographs, such as the wavy line for water and the triangle meaning "hilly country," "mountain," or "foreign country" in Babylonia and Sumer, had the same meaning than in Egypt. The snake is found in Egyptian and in Asiatic representation, but sometimes is hard to distinguish from the "n" sign. Perhaps this sign was originally a serpent, a plausible possibility in the word "eternity," "dt" in Egyptian, in which the wavy line is a determinative and not the letter "n." In a sealing from Abydos there is quite a selection of "ns" and serpents depicted. Perhaps originally the signs were different and the wavy lines for water were confused with the snakes in Egypt and in susa when they were taken into their respective scripts.

E.Baumgartel (1970) also does a review on the ivories from Abydos, where Petrie found a deposit with a quantity of objects in a room called M69 outside the temple of Dynasty IV and V. Among the objects was an ivory statuette of a woman, probably the wife or the daughter of King Aha from the First Dynasty. Other figurines also were found at Naqada, Helwan, Saqqara, and Tarkhan; most of these objects that date from Naqada II are at the Museum of the College of London. The importance of these finds is that they support the evidence that sculpture in the round was already achieved by the end of the Predynastic period since other bigger statues also were found at diverse Predynastic sites. For instance, many scholars think the colossus from Coptos discovered by Petrie (1986) may have had counterparts in Mesopotamian art. These colossi belonged to the early Naqada period; one of the statues is at the Cairo Museum and the others at the Ashmolean Museum in Oxford. The colossi present graffiti depicting a catfish, a serekh or palace facade, and a harpoon on the right leg. Williams

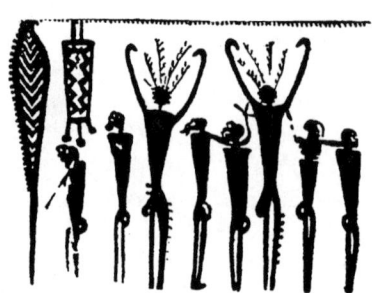

The Sacred Marriage
(Drawing by Alicia Meza)

(1988) did research on these colossi, and he affirms "the pharaonic culture was a well-developed monumental civilization by Dynasty O," which already had a large cult installation by this time. Williams compared these colossi with a striding statue found at Hierakonpolis and with other objects dating from the Naqada period, such as a kneeling statue found at the site of the main temple of Min and Isis at Coptos where the colossi were found. These two finds located at the same site may indicate all these statues were part of a structural complex rather than isolated monuments. This is more evidence for the monumental construction of the Naqada period.

For H.S. Smith the parallelism in Mesopotamian and Egyptian art representation is too strong to be culturally similar, and he prefers to call it "cultural interplay through trade" (1992:23-46). Sumer and Susa were centers where certain art style may have developed before than in Egypt. For instance, the motif of heroes dompteur is earliest attested at Susa I occupation in button seals and impressions, such as heroes taming lions and snakes vanquishing foes (fig. 1). In Egypt this motif is first seen in Tomb 100 at Hierakonpolis where a figure restrains two felines and at Naqada II another figure is macing three bounded, kneeling captives. The temple and palace facade appear in Uruk level IV a-b in archaic Susa sealings where above the paneled door are two lotuses intertwined, similar to lotus representations from Egypt. Processions also are shown carrying and bearing products similar to those processions from Egypt. A door is similar to the hieroglyphic sign G. 011; two birds on a door and a standard bearer result in the hieroglyphs "mh," G.V22, K3 and D28. Williams and Logan have shown that processions to the palace facade are a major element at Naqada III Royal cycle. Several representations of boat processions are depicted at tomb 100 and on knife handles from cemetery L at Qustul (1986). The floret motif, a symbol of heroes and the triumph over the forces of evil, also were found by Naqada IId-IIIb when the Egyptian kingship mythology was already in existence and the cultural influence was, perhaps, coming via another source.

As mentioned above, two possible sea routes were responsible for channeling all this exchange of information from Mesopotamia to Egypt. However, the inland route may have been used more frequently. Later, during Dynastic times, the route that preoccupied the Egyptians with security and control, was the border with Palestine that led the way into Syria and Mesopotamia.

At Em Besor, Israel, some seal impressions were recovered by the excavations of Tel Aviv University and published by Schulman from the City University of New York (1992). Ninety fragments from the First Dynasty or of Early Dynastic date were uncovered. Some of these fragments could have been part of envelopes for tokens since they are duplicated in other seal impressions that were found earlier. They all have Egyptian-style depictions on them. The petrographic analysis has proven that the mud used is

Palestinian clay and not Egyptian Nile mud. Therefore, according to Schulman, these fragments are from Canaan and of Egyptian manufacturing, indicating a probable Egyptian post in Palestine. Although these sealings were used and discarded in the area situated on the route from Mesopotamia to Egypt, Schulman argues that the making, use, and discarding of these impressions were local activities. They were probably discarded objects from people living in the area and not from transitory middlemen in their journey to trade; nor do the objects represent an Egyptian military dominance in Palestine. Evidence of Egyptian king names on seals meant a permanent Egyptian presence there, perhaps a border-control post or checkpoint.

Undoubtedly, Palestine also played a role in Egyptian Predynastic cultural symbiosis since Palestinian-style vessels also were found within early archaeological contexts. If, as is proposed by Porada, cylinder seals were a subdevelopment of the stone-vessel manufacture, the exchange of pottery-style manufacture between Mesopotamia and Egypt may have been a preliminary exchange of information for cylinder-seal manufacture. Stone vessels are earliest at Naqada I, and Egyptian stone vessels were found in Mesopotamia and in Iran. The stone used in the manufacture of these vases was not from Mesopotamia since this kind of stone was not from that area. The implication of these facts is that either the vases or the stone had to be imported. It seems that at Al Ubaid the stone vases were made of diorite, alabaster, white limestone, brecciated grey limestone, serpentine, and steatite—all raw materials found within Egypt (Collon, 1987:16-135).

Where Was the Influence for Social Complexity Coming From?

F. Hassan (1992) attributes the evolution of the Egyptian state to the outcome of several events occurring in different stages: stratification that occurred among Saharan herdsmen; the economic integration of neighboring villages; the emergence of leaders; the competition for prestige goods; the conflict between farming villages; the emergence of warriors; and the shift from a goddess cult associated with vegetation and focused on birth, death, and resurrection to a cosmogony of divine kingship.

If, as Hassan proposes, stratification first occurred among the Saharan herdsmen, his idea would be backed up by Sweyden's studies on the role buffaloes and bulls had during the Predynastic period in the Egyptian Sahara (1992). The long-horn buffalo was of African origin and during 7000 B.C. it was already appearing in the Egyptian Sahara. Later at about 4000 B.C. it was distributed along the Nile Valley when it gave the basis for the Apis bull cult. We have seen that cattle culture was important to Africans and that the two major deities associated with fertility during the Predynastic period, Selket and Hathor, were associated with the scorpion and the cow's horns, respectively. Min's association with fertility and his reference as "the bull of his mother" also is indication of the importance cattle symbolism already had during Predynastic times. If social stratification first occurred among Saharan herdsmen, this fact also could fit into the framework of an early Mesopotamian contact since herdsmen were connected with the pastoralists and nomads, who were referred to as the middlemen of the early long-range trade between Egypt, Mesopotamia, and India.

If originally there was a female fertility cult in Egypt, this proposal also may fit with the data available that there also was a female fertility cult in Mesopotamia (Baumgartel, 1966): the rosette being associated with the great goddess of fertility and the scorpion with motherhood. The goddess Isis, who later also was associated with Hathor and the cow's horns, had a prominent position in the Egyptian pantheon.[20] The association of Min and Osiris with vegetation and fertility also attests to an original relationship with a female goddess of fertility. A binary opposition was created: female-male, which, according to Hassan, had its epitome in the god Atum, the primordial god and creator.[21] The strong association of creation with sexuality is indicated in the linkage of divine kingship with sexuality. Min is an ithyphallic god, and Osiris is represented with his body in an ithyphallic position as well as his symbol, the djet pillar.

Early accounts of the struggle between Horus and Seth reveal the importance sex had in Egyptian cosmology.[22] Abnormal behavior is highlighted by using the opposition between male-female and the relationship between Horus and Seth. These accounts are written and described in diverse ancient Egyptian texts, such as the Book of the Dead. Hassan uses them to support his idea of an original binary opposition between female-male that shifted into an all-male cult through the reinforcement of the fertility goddess cult. By appropriating Seth's testicles, Horus became the sole king of Egypt, and if Seth was associated with the kings of Naqada and Horus with those of Hierakonpolis, the processes of unification may have been represented in the struggle between these two gods, explaining the rise of the state as multiple events. For Hassan the unification may have been the result of different struggles between centers which may have occurred about 3200 B.C.

If we consider Hassan's observations as feasible and correlate them with other events that may have occurred much earlier than 3200 B.C.–craft specialization, long-range trade, and cultural interaction with Mesopotamia; the fact that Egypt may already had developed an early marking communication system to support a trade network; monumental construction; and a cosmogony system—we are in the position of being able to test a much earlier state formation than that proposed by Hassan.

Evidence for early social stratification in the Nile Valley comes from Qustul in Nubia. According to Williams (1980; 1986), the A group from Khor Bahan had pottery identical to that of Naqada I. Although Naqada II imports were rare, Amratian occupation spread all the way to Wadi El Alaqui in the Sayala region (fig. 10).[23] There is evidence that Khor Daud had intensive trading with Egypt. The rich tombs found in Nubia provided evidence for political organization and class distinction in the form of status symbol objects, such as gold mace-handles and slate palettes.

Cemetery L at Qustul was an outstanding site with evidence of detectable changes in material culture and in political and social organization. Naqada I was contemporaneous with early A group phases Ib-IIa at Khor Bahan, and Naqada II-painted pottery with convex, wavy handles was contemporaneous with early A group IIa-c. Three types of burials were found at Qustul. The large tombs of cemetery L were similar to the large tomb from Hierakonpolis. A smaller version of this type of burials was found at Sayala and at Hierakonpolis; a style that also was shared by Naqada I and the early group A. All these tombs were probably part of complexes. The incense burners found there depict mat and post structures of the type used in cult centers' and royal tombs' construction in Egypt (fig. 2). The other two groups of tombs were smaller, but they were distinguished by their wealth.

Techniques and styles in pottery making that were shared among various groups in Nubia also were shared with some of the earlier phases of Tasian-Badarian and Naqada pottery. However, during Middle Naqada more complex methods for firing were introduced into Egypt and later entered the export flow to Nubia and Asia. Among the most interesting vessels found at cemetery L were jugs with shapes typical of the Early Bronze Age pottery in the Levant. Curiously, these shapes were not yet known from Egypt, and they present evidence of trade, perhaps via Palestine and the Red Sea. Incense burners showing the palace facades and serekhs with high-sterned sacred barks, which are all Egyptian depictions, also were among the objects found at cemetery L.

One of the incense burners was decorated with a recessed silouhette technique that can be related to rock art; others were incised with decorations in cylindrical bands (fig. 2). These decorations presented three vessels made in the shape of pharaonic sacred barks proceeding in a row to a palace facade. The vessels had ancillary signs and figures similarly arranged as those from the Naqada period. This burners' decoration style is related to the painted tomb 100 at Hierakonpolis. A post firing pot-mark is shown on a black topped vessel with a flat hull. The prow and the stern are bent upward, and a throne is placed amid ships; a small figure in a white robe is holding a flail and is seated on a raised seat under a canopy near the stern. This type of depiction, used during Narmer times, has been

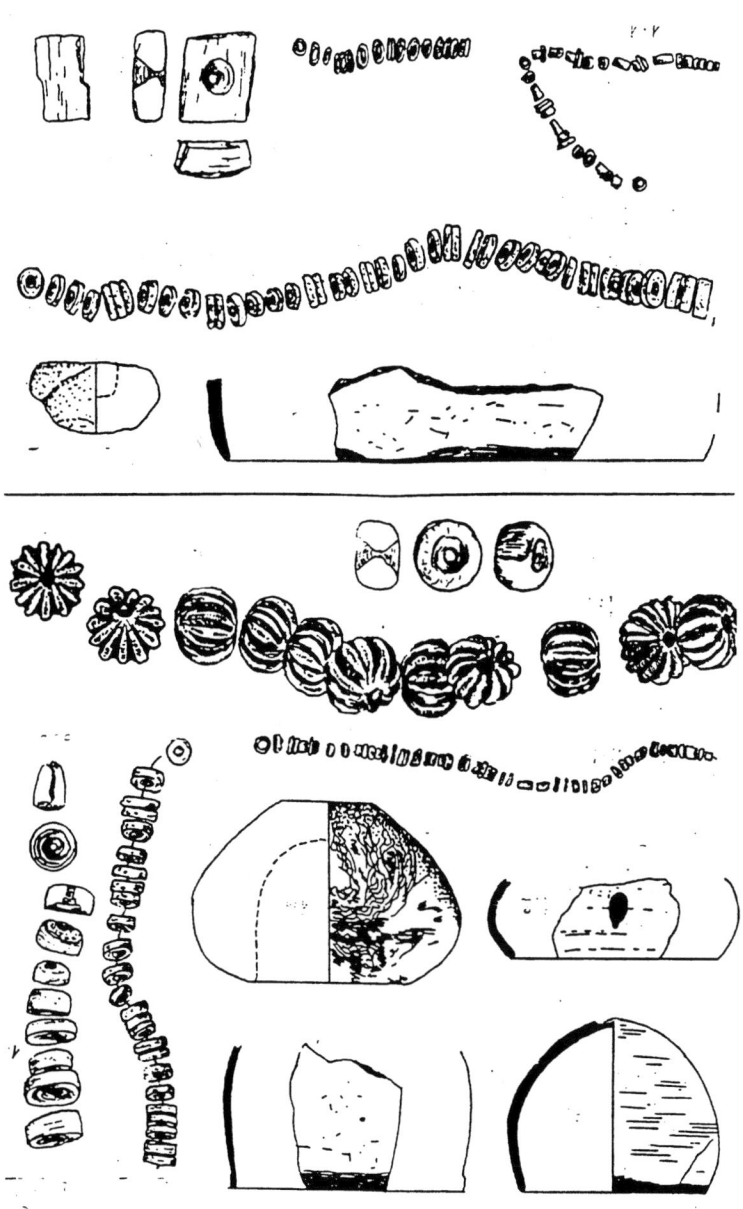

The Sayala Seals
(Drawing by Alicia Meza)

associated with pharaonic and religious functions and it is known to have been used later for funerary purposes.

The third bark has a falcon standard and next to it there is a feline with a pointed muzzle and pointed ears with its tail above its body.[24] A fish depicted below may be identified as a hieroglyph since it is used later as such. A man is standing with an upraised arm and he has a flap on his garment, identified as the type of dress worn by royal attendants in charge of royal documents. The man's beard is protruding from his face and resembles the Naqada II-III and Dynasty O representations. The next bark has the depiction of an antelope, a harpoon, and a pharaoh with the white crown of Upper Egypt. Resting on the serekh is the falcon and the rosette, which also occurs on a seal from Faras. On the bark there is a prisoner with bound arms behind his back guarded by a man who stands behind him armed with a mace and who also has a cord in his hand. This ceremony also is depicted during Naqada II-III. These depictions are part of a killing prisoners' ceremony and Heb Sed festival, which was the festival of renewal of kinship celebrated every thirty years during a king's reign.

The marks found on pottery were some fired before and others after the incision and decoration were made. The incisions were identification marks which were a combination of lines and hieroglyphs of Egyptian representation and also local. Two kinds of marks were simple, another was common in Nubia but rare in Egypt, such as humans, birds, animals, and complex linear or geometric designs. Inscriptions made on labels included prefiring incised groups, such as a falcon on a rectangle found in a jar. This is similar to an Egyptian inscription found in a royal tomb from Abydos. Kaiser translated this inscription as reading "Iry-Hor"; similarly, Williams translates the Qustul jar inscription as reading "Pe-Hor" since the rectangle may stand for the letter "p." Other signs shown on mace-heads and stone vessels are "scorpion" and "mountain." These filling motifs are common in Gerzean and Naqada II paintings as well as in Nubian pottery. The representation of progressive events also is a motif found on cylinder seals from Qustul with incised figures and with carved figures that resemble rock drawings also as those from the burners. Although the representations are culturally linked to the Naqada II period in Egypt, they also present a local imprint and, curiously, they also are indirectly related to Mesopotamian art depiction: vultures taming serpents and victory scenes painted on vessels and carved on ivory objects are all familiar motifs to Mesopotamian art. Although the development of writing also is attested in Nubia at this time, writing's influence on the cultural development of this area was not as important as it was in Egypt.

Conclusions

I will review here the main points formulated in the last chapters in order to substantiate the hypothesis proposed at the beginning of this thesis. Archaeological evidence indicates that: (1) Predynastic towns proliferated throughout Egypt from Buto in the Delta to Qustul and Sayala in Nubia; (2) some of these towns developed into large centers interspersed with less large centers and small towns and villages, integrating in a four-level hierarchical system (see histogram); (3) the possibilities for these towns to increase in size and importance depended on the movement of peoples from one town to another and on how centers competed with each other for trade routes and source of materials, developing full-time craft specialists and production monopolization; (4) sources for procuring raw materials and the distribution of goods depended on how information was being channeled and how this information was used to create social stratification (Johnson); and (5) the social development of Predynastic Egypt was similar to the social development occurring in Warka and Susa throughout the fourth millennium B.C. There is at this time archaeological evidence for incipient social stratification in diverse centers throughout the Nile Valley area (Bard, Fairsevis, Harlan, Griswold).

The philological evidence suggests that: (1) the marking system used to convey information in Predynastic Egypt was employed by most of the Predynastic towns, a factor indicative that the Predynastic towns were trading with each other; (2) the correspondence Egyptian markings had with Mesopotamian markings on tokens suggests an information exchange may have occurred between the two regions; (3) labels and seals with Mesopotamian designs were found throughout Egypt from Abydos and Hierakonpolis in Upper Egypt to Sayala in Nib (Bietak); (4) if the cones found by von der Way in Buto are related to the Mesopotamian system, the complete area of the Nile valley can be comprised within a regional exchange system; and (5) the archaeological context for the Egyptian finds, such as temple deposits and elite graves, is similar to the archeological context for the Mesopotamian tokens.

Evidence of Mesopotamian influence on Egyptian cultural development also has been demonstrated in the works of Baumgartel, Emery, and Williams. It also has been shown that there was a parallelism in the timing of Egyptian social development to that of Mesopotamia: the three main Predynastic periods divided into Badarian, 4000-3700 B.C.; Amratian, 3700-3500 B.C.; and Gerzean, 3500-3200 B.C. coincide with those of Mesopotamia, Ubaid, Terminal Susa A-early Uruk, middle Uruk, and late Uruk. According to Johnson, the Mesopotamian state developed at the beginning of the Middle Uruk period, and unfolded at about 3500 B.C. According to Harlan, Hierakonpolis was, at this time, monopolizing the production and distribution of ceramics. This monopoly involved the employment of full-time craft specialists under the control of growing elites, as it is attested by the standardization of ceramic production (Johnson). Not only Harlan but also Hoffman, Fairsevis, and Kaiser indicated earlier dates for social stratification at Hierakonpolis. Mortesen also corroborated dates for el Omari.

Although the evidence for the development of a counting system in Egypt is scarce and more research is needed, there are some elements which indicate that such a system was in use in Predynastic Egypt during the fourth millennium B.C. For instance, Schmandt-Besserat has indicated that some counters were displayed at the Cairo Museum (Johnson, personal communication) and I also have observed the same type of artifacts in display at the Cairo Museum in Egypt and the Metropolitan Museum of Art in New York. The counters at the Metropolitan Museum were some of the objects excavated by Petrie at Tarkhan and were obtained in an exchange with the British Museum. Although I have to corroborate if the objects mentioned above are really tokens, Susan Allen from the MMA informed me that the use of such counters was witnessed by her at Mendes, a site in the Delta, where pieces of pottery were modified even by modern Egyptians in order to use them as counters or as gaming pieces. This is a possible explanation for the presence of counters in the same context as the gaming pieces. Perhaps they were used also as such.

Since Mesopotamian tokens were associated with agriculture and with the storage of grain, it is not surprising that their archaeological contexts were the temple deposits: tokens were used for accounting and they were part of the redistributive economy of the temples. The same type of temple redistributive economy was employed in Ancient Egypt, where temples grew to acquire unprecedented economic and political power, and they constituted "the first great corporations of the ancient world" (Kees; Trigger).

There is philological evidence that Egypt, as Mesopotamia, had a counting system up to number "three," a number which also meant "many." This rudimentary counting system may have evolved into a more abstract and inclusive type of system which may have been able to express large quantities with only one written word.

Some scholars do not believe pot-marks or graffiti developed into hieroglyphs because they see the hieroglyphic system more connected to religious than economic purposes. However, there is evidence from the use of the proto-language reconstruction method in linguistics that languages always carry ancestral traits in their grammars and phonetics, no matter what transformations the language may have suffered (Bendix). In this way, a language can be traced to the place and time of the proto-language origin. Therefore, even if we admit that hieroglyphs were intimately related to religion, this fact does not exclude the possibility that traits from pot-marks and graffiti were used and adapted to new forms and meaning of words.

A correlation of marks in the appendix shows there is a correspondence of signs, graffiti, and pot-marks. It is not a perfect correlation because even within the same language, words had more than one meaning depending on context and sintax. Markings on tokens and pots, on graffiti and cuneiform, and on hieroglyphic signs all relate even if it is not in an exact way. Years ago Emery had already advanced the notion that there existed a correlation between pot-marks and hieroglyphs. If Mesopotamian seals, which developed out of a token system, developed into Egyptian scarabs used as seals (Gibson), it is not a fortuitous event. Van den Brink, who also has studied the Thinite pot-marks, indicates that, at this time, a grammatical system was already in progress using this rudimentary system of writing. It is not casual, either, the fact that some signs used as markings in the Mesopotamian token system were later found in Egypt used as hieroglyphs, such as the "niwt" sign for "town" and the "mw" sign used to designate "water" or "liquid."

Summarizing this evidence we see that, although not substantially proven, Egypt had a counter system and also had a regional system of interaction. Within this system, towns were being integrated in preparation for the consolidation of the inclusive Egyptian unification. Moreover, Egypt was a participant in an interregional system, as is demonstrated by the plotted rank-size distribution of Predynastic towns. Mesopotamia also was included within this interregional system through which both regions had contact and exchange. This factor is attested in the presence of raw materials and finished products in contexts that were not their origin. For instance, Egyptian alabaster vases were found in Mesopotamian sites. Silver and lapis lazuli were found in seals and artifacts of Mesopotamian origin in Egypt. This cultural and economic exchange allowed exchange of information through which new ideas diffused and were adapted. For instance, state formation in Egypt can be compared with the type of social development that occurred at Warka. The growth of the Warka system was dendritic with centers expanding and proliferating, sometimes absorbing other smaller centers, sometimes being included themselves into their neighbors' grip.

In the Nile Valley, Armant was an example of this type of social growth since Armant was a small growing town that existed between two other growing towns in the region, Hierakonpolis and Naqada. Griswold made a point when he indicated that Armant's failure to expand and to achieve social stratification was due to its geographical position between Naqada and Hierakonpolis, two large centers. Griswold indicated as Bard had observed, that only after the Egyptian unification was achieved and perhaps only by royal manipulation, was Armant allowed to grow and become stratified. This fact is an indication that the information provided by the rank-size settlement plot of Egyptian towns, given in the appendix, could have been a reality. Moreover, the way in which centers and towns were distributed and how they were proliferating indicates a dendritic system at work.

Interaction was becoming tighter with the growth of large centers. Subsequently, a growing participation in an outside system could be observed if the Egyptian and the Mesopotamian systems were correlated with each other. This last fact has yet to be proven, but, obviously, both systems were working into being integrated into an interregional system during the same time period.

In respect of social interaction, which also sometimes involves conflict, the little fortified towns shown on the Libyan palette are not just a depiction of local conflict and struggle, they are telling us something else: Egyptian states were developing. As Bard has advanced, this development may have occurred before 3200 B.C.

However, after all the evidence provided throughout this paper, I propose that: (1) Egyptian Predynastic towns were developing into pristine states by 3500 B.C., a development that was parallel to that of Mesopotamia; (2) Egypt at this time was being gradually integrated into a regional and an interregional system of exchange and interraction; (3) also during this period, Egypt was developing a writing system, a complex cosmology, and monumental construction. These developments involved a standardization of ceramic production with full-time specialists; (4) Egypt was achieving these accomplishments by incorporating Mesopotamian cultural traits into an African setting that later would result in the consolidation of the distinctive Egyptian character and culture; (5) state formation in Egypt was a gradual process without any possibility of shifting back into a less developed form of social organization. This state formation was an irreversible process; (6) Egyptian state formation was not an isolated event. It was a multiple process involving a dendritic system of settlements where growing centers were becoming small states; (7) the formation of these small states also may have involved conflict; and (8) as it was related in mythical accounts, the final chapter of this multi-state war ended with the unification of Upper and Lower Egypt during Naqada II at 3200 B.C.

Chronology

The dates used here are based on the chronology in Baines and Málek 1980, pp. 36–37.

Predynastic		5500–2920 BC
Badarian		5500–4000
Amratian (Naqada I)		4000–3500
Gerzean (Naqada II)		3500–3100
Late Predynastic (Naqada III)		3100–2920
Early Dynastic Period		2920–2649
1st Dynasty		2920–2770
2nd Dynasty		2770–2649
Old Kingdom		2649–2134
3rd Dynasty		2649–2575
Djoser (Netjerykhet) 2630–2611		
4th Dynasty		2575–2465
5th Dynasty		2465–2323
Raneferef 2419–2416		
6th Dynasty		2323–2150
7th/8th Dynasties		2150–2134
First Intermediate Period		2134–2040
9th/10th Dynasties		2134–2040
11th Dynasty (Theban)		2134–2040
Middle Kingdom		2040–1640
11th Dynasty		2040–1991
12th Dynasty		1991–1783
13th Dynasty		1783–after 1640
14th Dynasty		
Second Intermediate Period		1640–1532
15th Dynasty (the Hyksos)		
16th Dynasty (the lesser Hyksos)		
17th Dynasty		1640–1550
New Kingdom		1550–1070
18th Dynasty		1550–1307
Thutmose III	1479–1425	
Hatshepsut	1473–1458	
Amenhotep II	1427–1401	
Thutmose IV	1401–1391	
Amenhotep III	1391–1353	
Akhenaten	1353–1335	
Smenkhare	1335–1333	
Tutankhamun	1333–1323	
Ay	1323–1319	
Horemheb	1319–1307	
19th Dynasty		1307–1196
Ramesses I	1307–1306	
Seti I	1306–1290	
Ramesses II	1290–1224	
Merneptah	1224–1214	
20th Dynasty		1196–1070
Ramesses III	1194–1163	
Third Intermediate Period		1070–712
21st Dynasty		1075–945
Siamun	978–959	
22nd Dynasty		945–712
Shoshenq I	945–924	
Shoshenq II	909–883	
Shoshenq III	835–783	
23rd Dynasty		828–712
Iuput II	731–720	
24th Dynasty		724–712
25th Dynasty (Nubia + Theban area)		770–712
Kashta	770–750	
Piye	750–712	
Late Period		712–332
25th Dynasty (Nubia + all Egypt)		712–657
Taharka	690–664	
26th Dynasty		664–525
Psametik I	664–610	
Apries	589–570	
Amasis	570–526	
27th Dynasty (Persian)		525–404
28th Dynasty		404–399
29th Dynasty		399–380
30th Dynasty		380–343
Second Persian Period		343–332
Graeco-Roman Period		332 BC–AD 395
Ptolemaic Period		332 BC – 30 BC
Ptolemy I	304–284	
Roman period		30 BC–AD 395
Meroitic Kingdom		300 BC–AD 350

Appendix

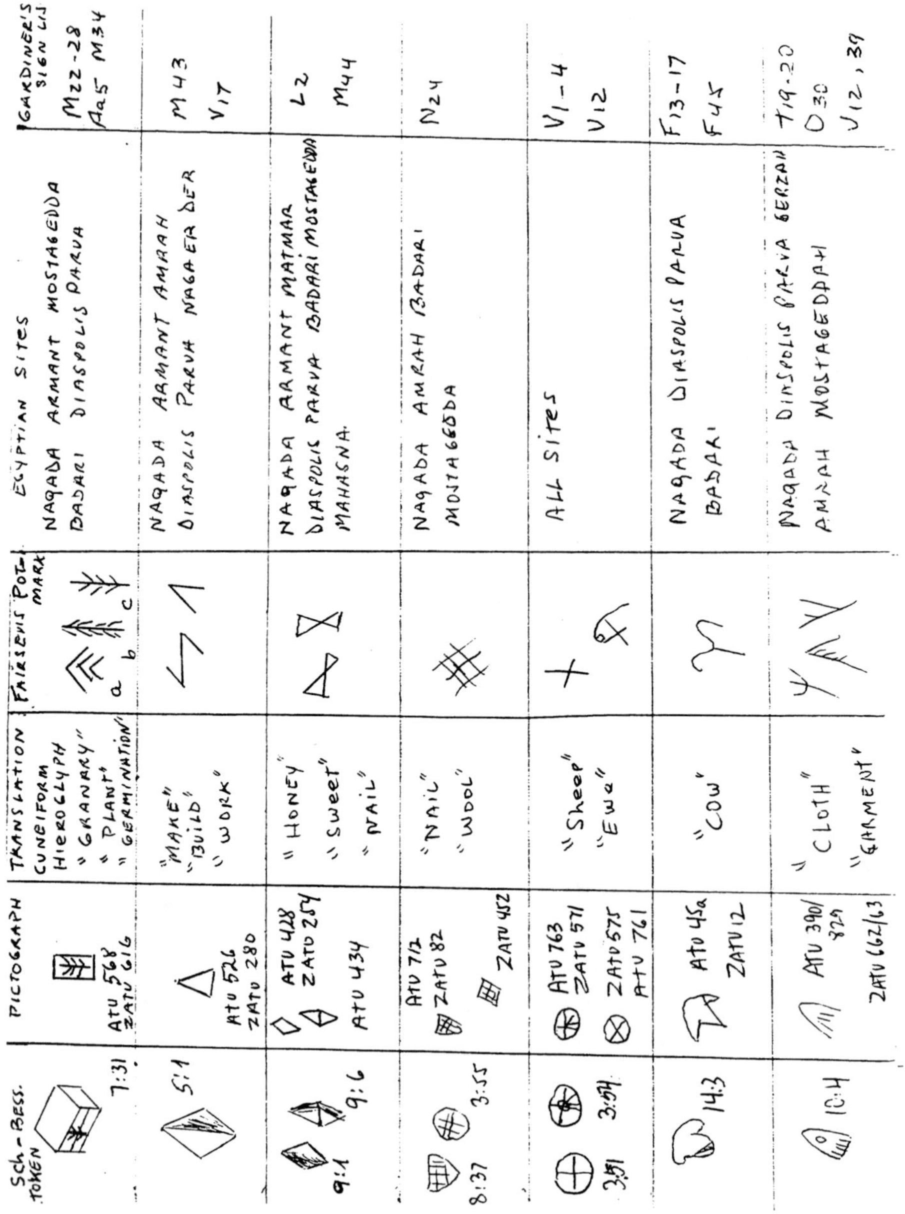

Sch-Bess. Token	Pictograph	Translation Cuneiform Hieroglyph	Fairlew's Pot Mark	Egyptian Sites	Gardiner's Sign List
7:31	ATU 568 ZATU 616	"Granary" "Plant" "Germination"	(a, b, c marks)	Naqada Armant Mostagedda Badari Diaspolis Parva	M22-28 Aa5 M34
5:1	ATU 526 ZATU 280	"Make" "Build" "Work"		Naqada Armant Amrah Diaspolis Parva Nagaed Der	M43 V17
9:1 9:6	ATU 428 ZATU 284 ATU 434	"Honey" "Sweet" "Nail"		Naqada Armant Matmar Diaspolis Parva Badari Mostagedda Mahasna	L2 M44
8:37 3:55	ATU 712 ZATU 82 ZATU 452	"Nail" "Wool"		Naqada Amrah Badari Mostagedda	N24
3:31 3:54	ATU 763 ZATU 571 ZATU 675 ATU 761	"Sheep" "Ewe"		All Sites	V1-4 V12
14:3	ATU 45a ZATU 12	"Cow"		Naqada Diaspolis Parva Badari	F13-17 F45
10:4	ATU 390/329 ZATU 662/663	"Cloth" "Garment"		Naqada Diaspolis Parva Berzah Amrah Mostagedda	T19-20 O30 V12, 39

Fig. 1
(Drawing by Alicia Meza)

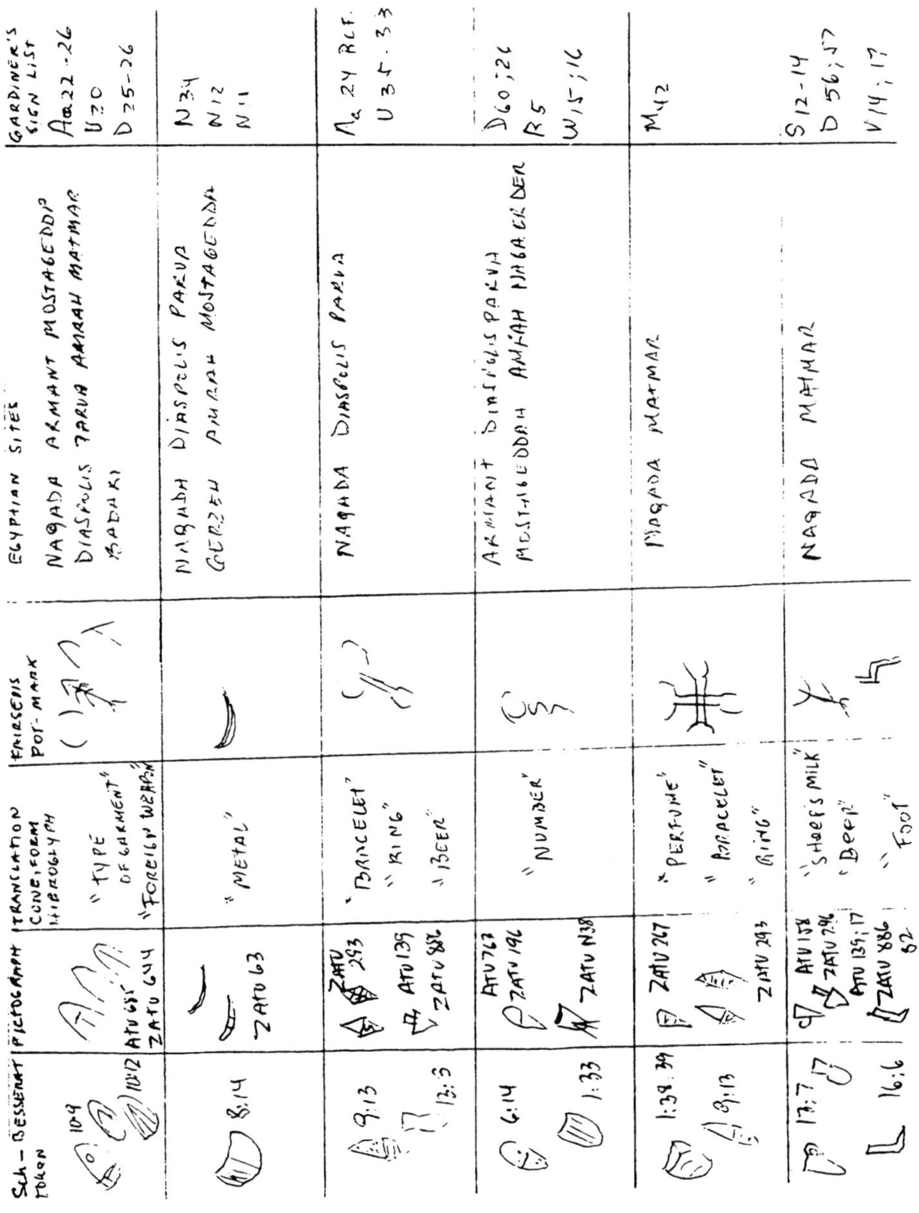

Sch-Bessenat Token	Pictograph	Translation Cuneiform Hieroglyph	Proto-Ellis Pot-Mark	Egyptian Sites	Gardiner's Sign List
104	ATU 651 ZATU 644 10½	"TYPE OF GARMENT" "FOREIGN WOMAN"	( )	NAGADA ARMANT MOSTAGEDDI? DIASPOLIS PARVA AMRAH MATMAR KADARI	Aa22-26 U20 D25-26
8.14	ZATU 63	"METAL"		NAQADH DIASPOLIS PARVA GERZEH AMRAH MOSTAGEDDA	N34 N12 N11
9.13 13:3	ZATU 293 ATU 139 ZATU 88L	"BRACELET" "RING" "BEER"		NAGADA DIASPOLIS PARVA	Aa 24 Ref. U 34-33
6.14 1.33	ATU 763 ZATU 19L ZATU N38	"NUMBER"		ARMANT DINISPOLIS PARVA MOSTAGEDDA AMRAH NAGA EL DER	D60;26 R5 W15;16
1.39, 39 13:13	ZATU 247 ZATU 293	"PERFUME" "BRACELET" "RING"		NAGADA MATMAR	M42
13:7 16:6	ATU 138 ZATU 29L ATU 139;17 ZATU 886 S2	"SHOE'S MILK" "BEEF" "FOOT"		NAGADA MATMAR	S12-14 D56;57 V14;17

Fig. 2
(Drawing by Alicia Meza)

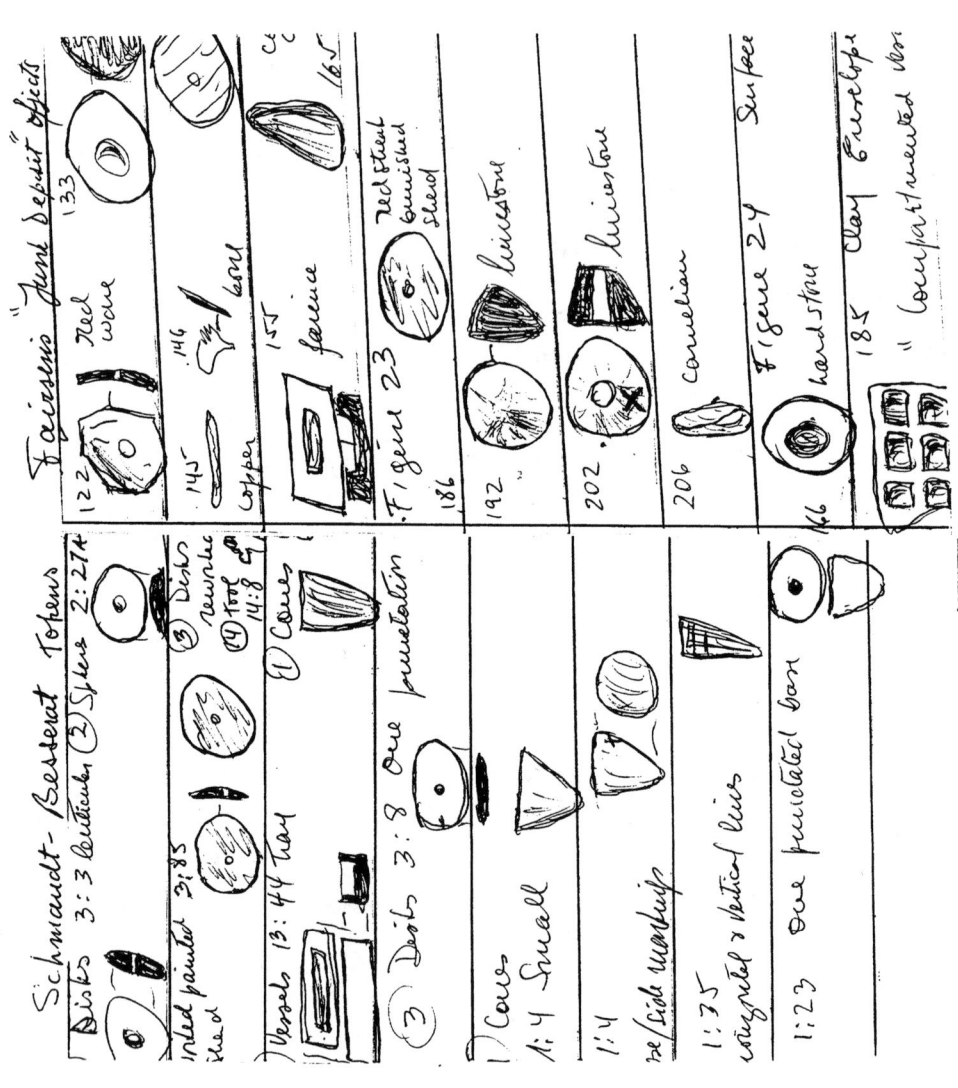

Fig. 3
(Drawing by Alicia Meza)

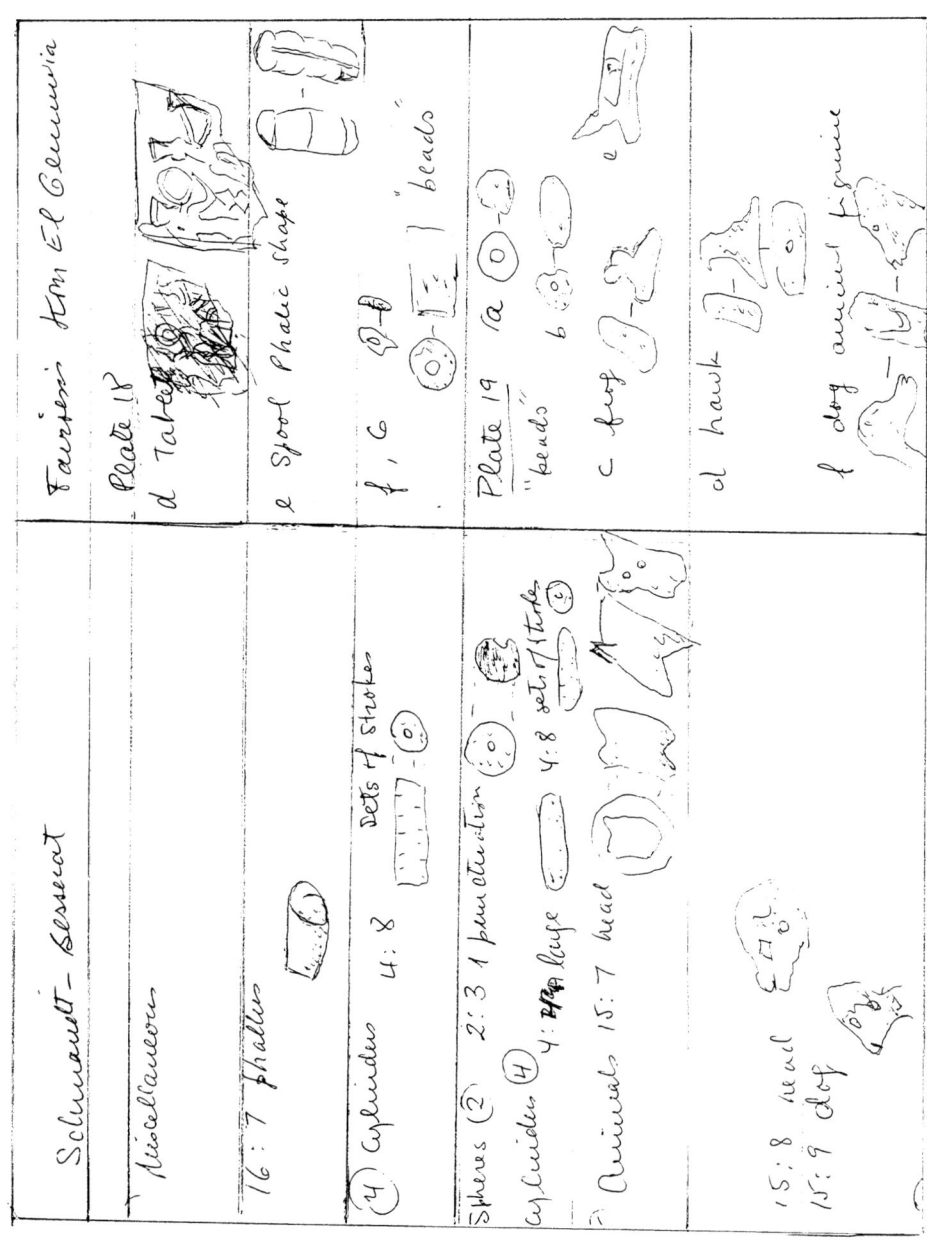

Fig. 4
(Drawing by Alicia Meza)

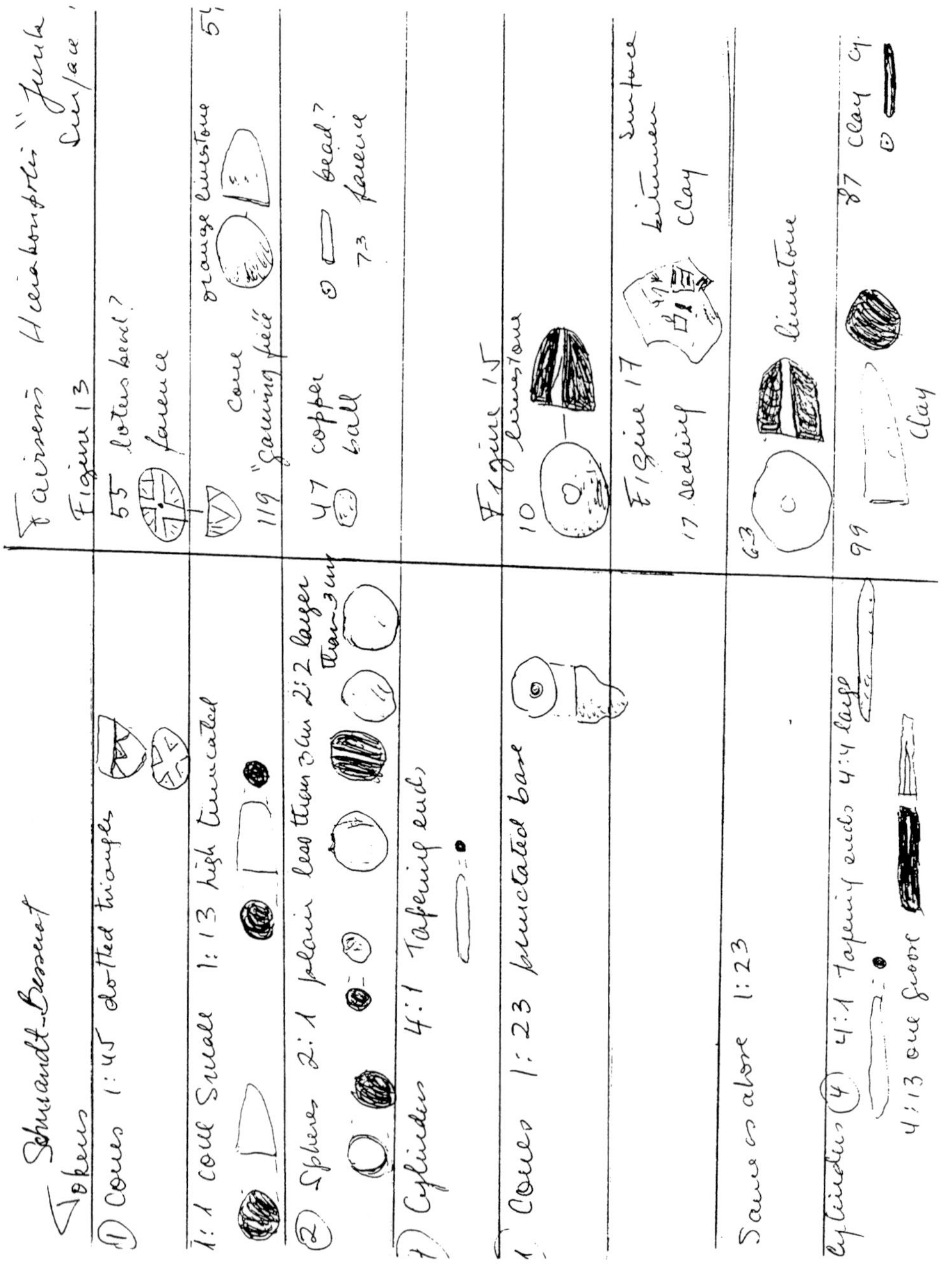

Fig. 5
(Drawing by Alicia Meza)

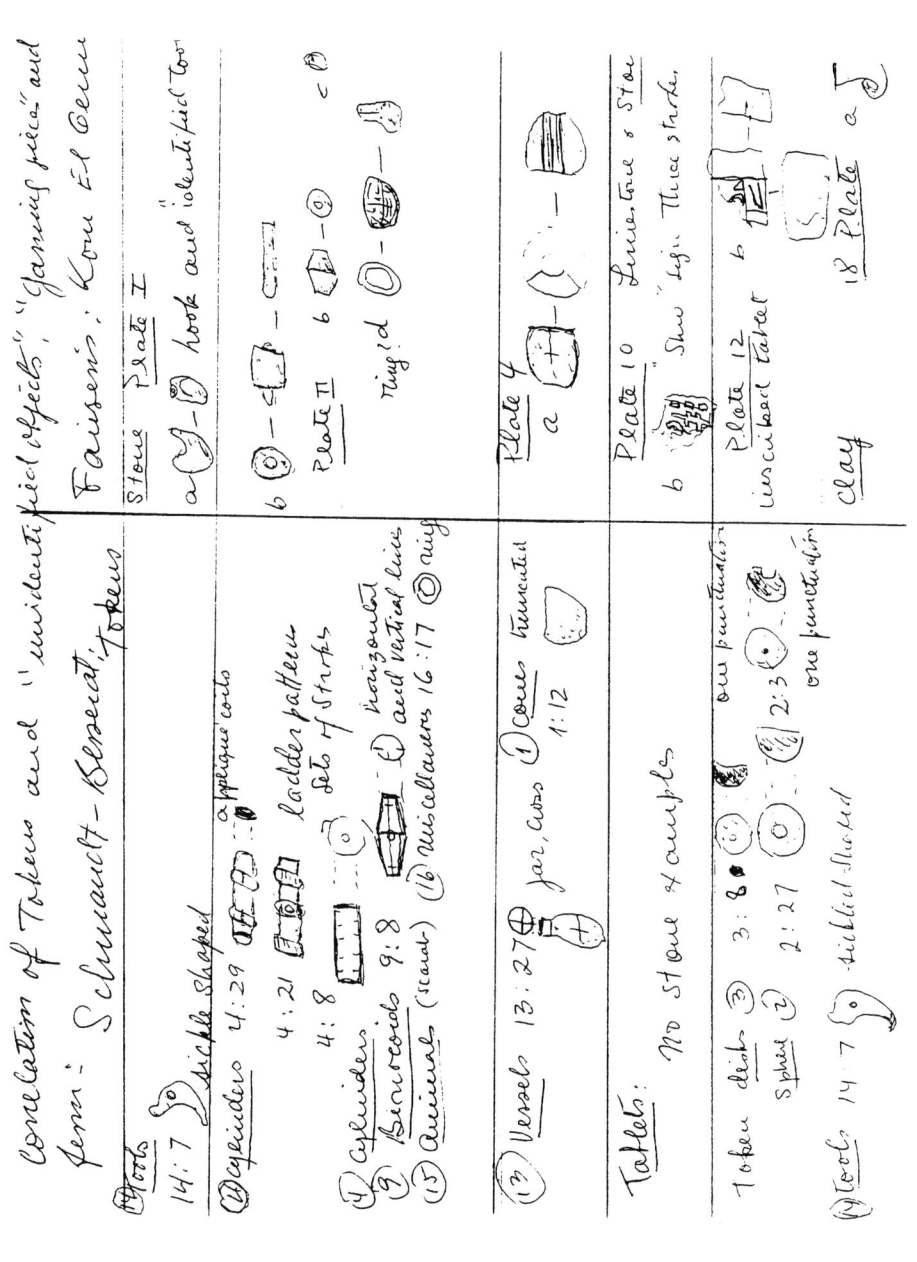

Fig. 6
(Drawing by Alicia Meza)

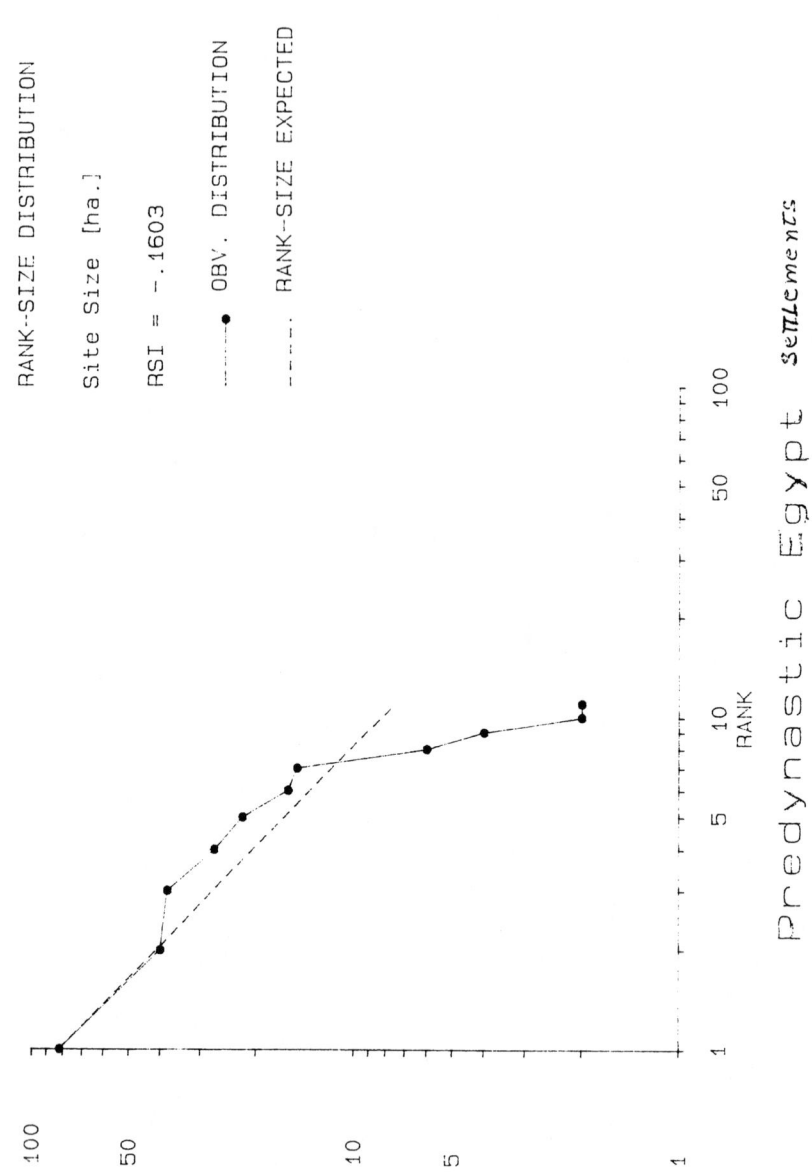

Fig. 7
(Graphs by Gregory Johnson)

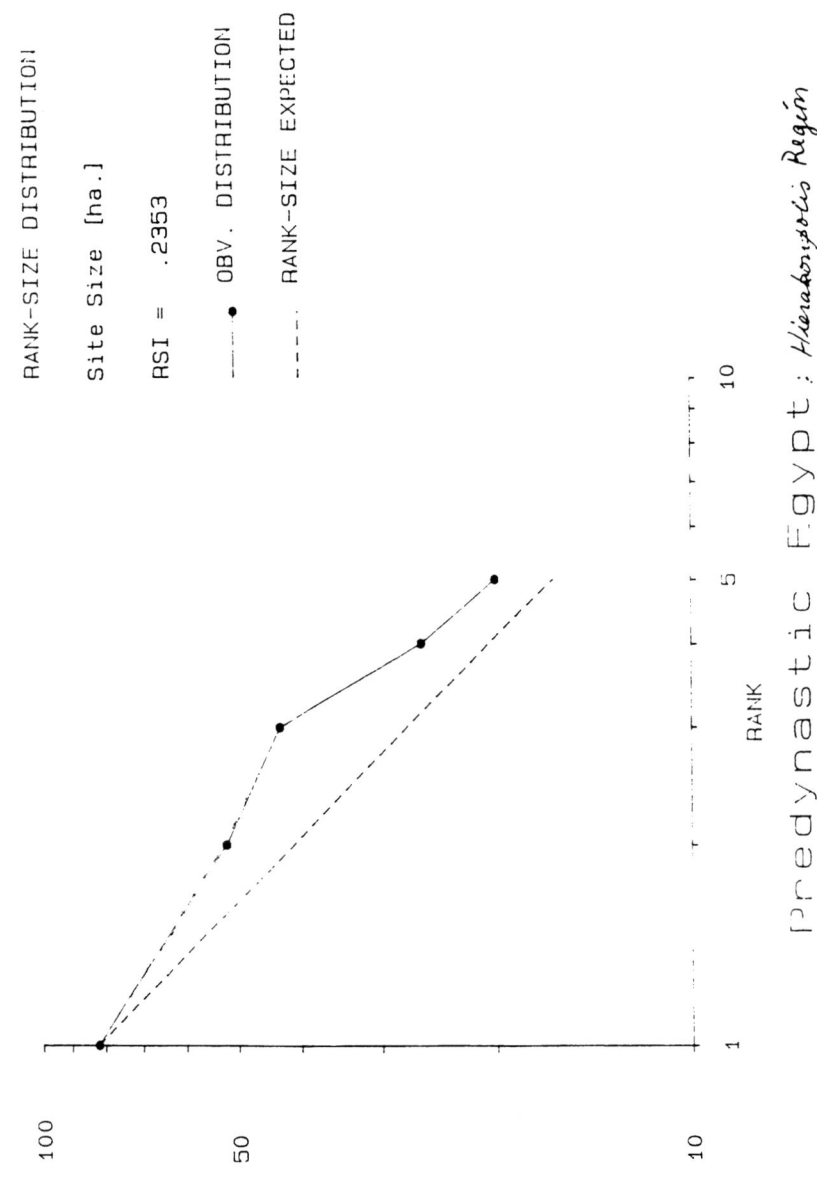

Fig. 8
(Graphs by Gregory Johnson)

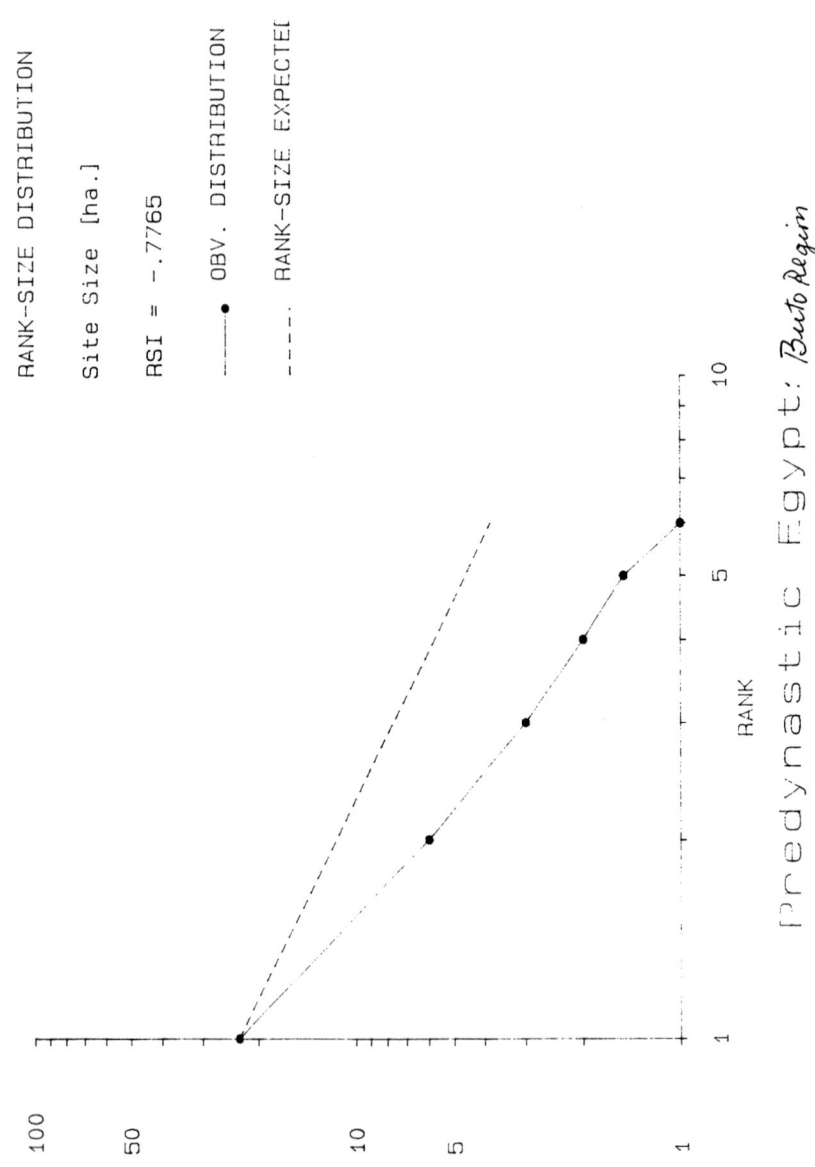

Fig. 9
(Graphs by Gregory Johnson)

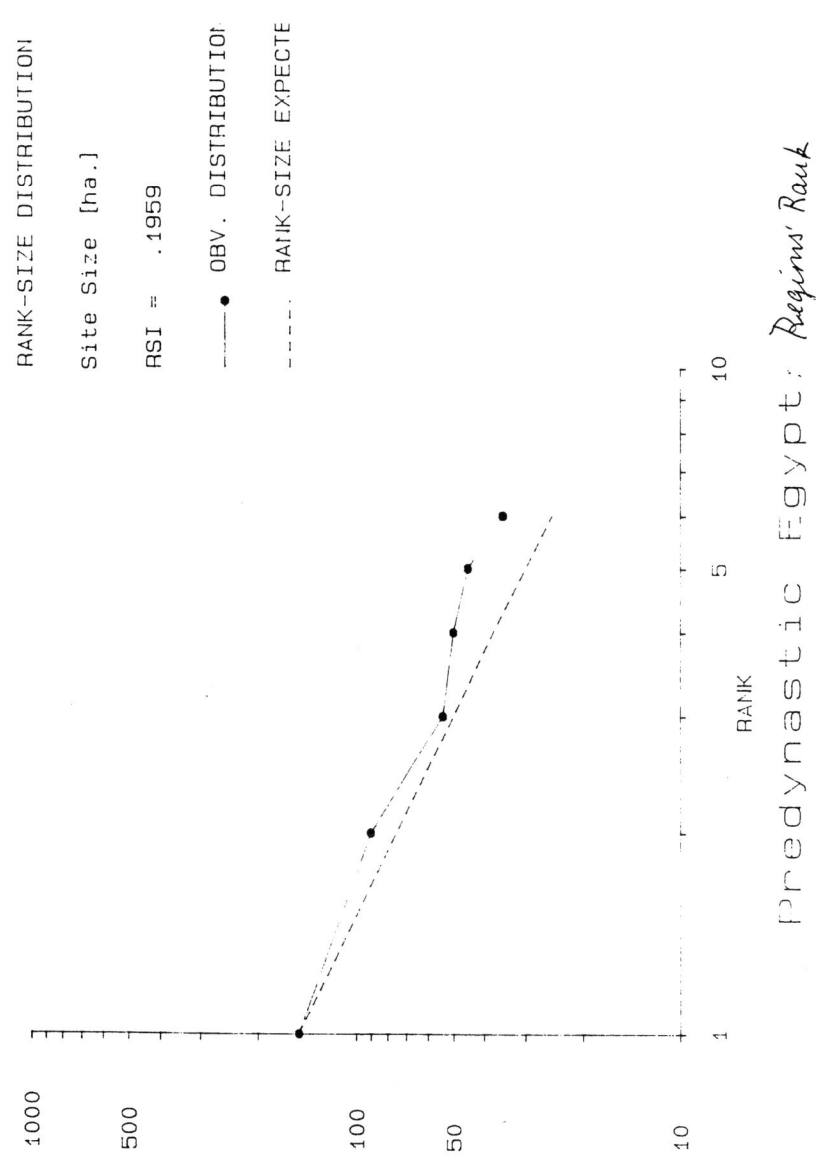

Fig. 10
(Graphs by Gregory Johnson)

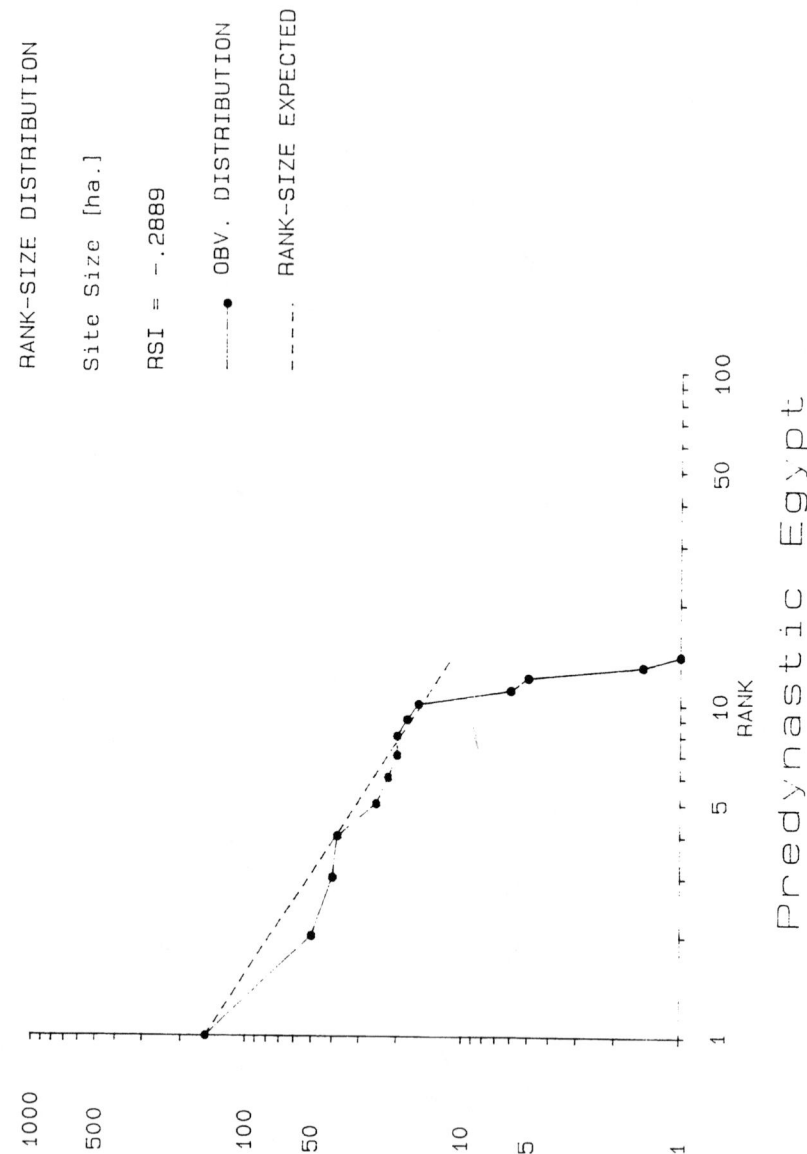

Fig. 11
(Graphs by Gregory Johnson)

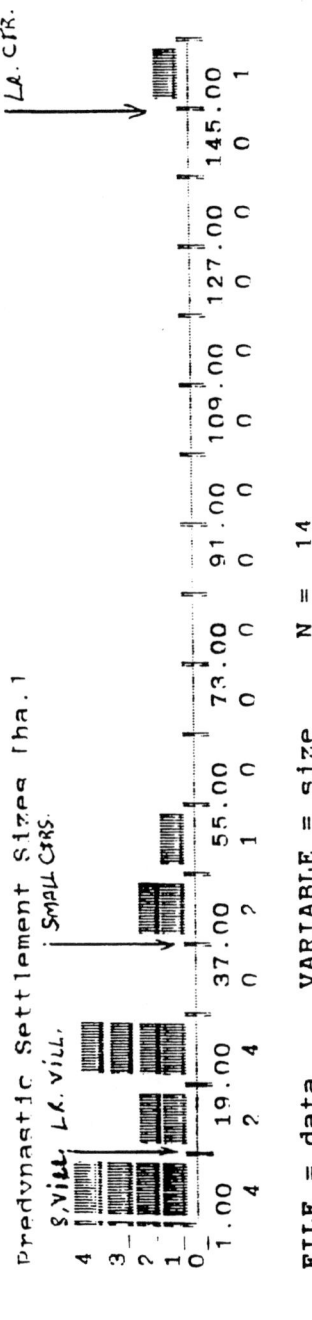

Fig. 12
(Graphs by Gregory Johnson)

End Notes

1. Schmandt-Besserat distinguishes between a concrete system of counting by representing a unit of an item with each simple token and an abstract system of reckoning things in which diverse marks or formats do not necessarily represent one item of its kind. Different formats, incisions, and perforations led to an abstract system to reckon things, such as numbers and signs to identify quality, and provenance of merchandise (Schmandt-Besserat, 1992: 192).
2. Although the Egyptian structures are not an exact copy of the Mesopotamian walls, the exterior niches of the Egyptian Predynastic enclosures resemble Mesopotamian temples of the early Ubaid Period, a style that lasted within the regional architectural tradition. In Egypt this type of niche paneling ceased to be by the Second Dynasty. This observation was also made by Frankfort, who also believes in a Mesopotamian influence in the origin of Egyptian writing (Trigger, 1983:37 and footnote). See also Fischer, 1990:61-62 and footnote No. 14.
3. Grave volume is a significant variable for assessing social status and possible social stratification. Lorenz curve plots the cumulative proportion of a variable against the cumulative proportion of the population. Cases are rank ordered from lowest to highest and the proportion of the total held by that rank are calculated; a line / means perfect equality among societies; the further the line dips below the line of equality, the greater the inequality. The Gini index is defined in terms of the Lorenz curve; it measures the area between the line of perfect equality and the actual line. The Gini index is equal to twice the area between these two lines; it allows inequality to be invariant to proportionate increases or decreases in everyone's score. This means that if all graves increased in volume by 20% between periods the Gini index would not be affected. The numerical expression ranges from zero to one, which is complete inequality.

    Griswold indicates that enough evidence cannot be extracted to prove inequality just by comparing tomb volume, since increase in volume may mean just more preoccupation with providing for the dead. Using one variable is not accurate to assess social status. Other factors, such as dress, body position, number of articles deposited in the grave, and the position of the individual within the cemetery are also important status assessment factors. Grave volume correlates well with those burials of individuals that seem to have been special because they are associated with status symbols such as in the case of the Second Dynasty tombs.

They also correlate well with monumental architecture of later periods. Lorenz curves and Gini indexes are well suited to assess inequality within in societies.

4. "nn" may indicate ownership since "n" is a sign indicating possession; "of" may be here referring to a person. Another possibility is that "nn" may also be part of the determinative of the word for "drink" "liquid." A second alternative is that the "n" sign sometimes replaces the sign for land, which in this case may represent "provenance" (Gardiner, 1982:490).

5. In pp. 219 von der Way indicates that these nails are similar to those from Uruk culture. Johnson, (personal communication) indicates that these objects are not nails but cones, and they are not of Uruk style but Ubaid.

6. Johnson, (personal communication), indicates that these finds are not Middle Uruk but Late Uruk period.

7. According to the "Central Place Theory," this development of centers in a settlement system occurs when people living near a main site meet at this central place to trade, worship, and deposit produce in temples and warehouses. A leadership develops in what could be classified as a two-tier settlement system in which centers may compete for clients and the monopoly of production and distribution of goods that still lead these centers into a further development and subsequently to a four-tier settlement system. From the position, size and type of these settlements, information about their spatial relationships, and centrality of organizational structures can be inferred, according to Johnson: "Interaction among settlements varies inversely with some function of distance and directly with some function of sizes of the interacting populations" (1977:480-501) "Centralization is the expression of hierarchical subordination; the degree of centralization depends on the degree of the development of a settlement system." Several methods can be used to measure social interaction among settlements, such as ceramic style similarity and distribution of goods for which location of production is known, although similar distribution patterns may result from a variety of exchange mechanisms (1988-1989).

8. This system of simple tokens was a concrete mode of counting merchandise. One counter or token stood for each single specific type of the item to be counted. Tokens were generally made of baked clay and Besserat classified them into sixteen different types, according to shapes, and about five hundred subtypes, according to size or additional markings. Plain tokens were mostly restricted to cones, spheres, disks, cylinders, and tetrahedrons and had a plain surface (Schmandt-Besserat 6, 13, 360).

9. Stone tokens present a great variety of types of stone and color. For instance, they were made of pink, green, or black marble, white

alabaster, grey slate, brown sandstone, or reddish ocher. These stone tokens were mostly produced in northern Mesopotamia, bitumen tokens were mostly produced in southern Mesopotamia and the Susiana Plain of western Iran; plaster was occasionally found in Turkey (Schmandt-Besserat, 1992:29-30).

10. The system of marking on envelopes introduced a new phase in the token system: the impressed tablets, which replaced the envelopes containing tokens. These impressed signs still represented the shape of tokens but they assumed a new function since they replaced the device of marking envelopes on the surface and matching it with the tokens placed inside the envelope. The message on the tablets was "the message" (Schmandt-Besserat, 1992:129).

11. This assertion from Schmandt-Besserat agrees with the actual research of Historical Linguistics that uses the proto-word method for tracing languages origins and for the reconstruction of prehistory, since always languages preserve vocabulary and form in their evolution throughout time (Edward Bendix, December 3, 1993 lecture at Hunter College, CUNY). Also see Schmandt-Besserat, 1992, 184-86.

12. Johnson, in a personal communication, also mentioned these warfare scenes depicted on seals, but he does not agree on a possible domination of Elam by Sumer. He thinks these scenes just reflect warfare among centers.

13. In John Baines, "Literacy, Social Organization, and the Archaeological Record: The Case of Early Egypt," *State and Society. The Emergence and Development of Social Hierarchy and Political Centralization,* ed. by J. Gledhill, B. Bender and M. T. Larsen (London 1988:192-214).

14. Instead, Fairsevis says that in south Asian archaeology, sites are treated as units separately; in this way it is easier to detect any changes in social organization within each unit, and to develop valid theoretical notions of state origin and development; a fatal gap in Egyptian archaeology and anthropological theory concerning early Egypt state formation. Fairsevis indicates that whatever the ordering of artifact assemblages it does not mean that ordering at one site is the same for all sites, since sometimes ceramics that are of later date may be intrusive to an earlier strata. For instance, the evidence is not the same if it is coming from settlements, from temples or if it is mortuary where intrusions to an earlier strata is more possible than in settlements or temples. Hierakonpolis presents settlements and temple occupation, instead in Armant and in Diaspolis Parva, all the evidence comes from burials.

15. Harlan (1985) gives a description of Hierakonpolis settlements beginning with their datings. For instance, he believes that locality 11c may have been occupied from the Amratian to the Gerzean period, between 3790 B.C. and locality 29, between 3680 to 3550 B.C., which corresponds to the Amratian period. Hassan has referred to the Khattara settlement

as a Badarian site, and Naqada as a Gerzean, but recently, he has reconsidered Khattara as Naqada I, early Naqada II; and Naqada, as Naqada II. Although these dates may be accurate for specific points in time, according to Harlan, settlements may bridge different cultural periods, making it difficult to date them to a determinate time period. For Harlan, increasing social stratification is a documented phenomena separating the Amratian and Gerzean periods as it is indicated by the arrival of new wares and differences in tomb sizes that may mean social changes.

16. Harlan adds that site function may explain variances obtained in testing, the greater the variances the different of uses for pots of a particular shape. From the test of homogeneity and coefficient of variation, there is not compelling evidence of standardized pottery production, but Harlan explains that in cases where larger and temporarily more dispersed samples are obtained, there is a higher index of frequency of shapes. This higher index occurs at locality 34, which Harlan thinks is attributable to the presence of special inhabitants on site, such as an elite, a fact corroborated by the architectural remains. A variation on incisions on vessels also coincides with the transition of the Amratian-Early Gerzean periods.

17. Besides class of interaction, size of interacting population is the other variable employed in a gravity model used for studying interacting populations. Distance has different effect on the distribution of the different types of artifacts. For instance, a group of interacting populations may contain a high number of low status items while a second group of populations may contain higher number of high status items, indicating that this group may contain elites. Some raw materials with utilitarian uses for a certain population may well represent a high status item for others, depending on the decreasing availability with distance from source, such as in the case of obsidian (Johnson, 1977).

18. Distance, according to Johnson, may also be measured in terms of costs of movement or travel time. By increasing sedentarization, exploiting environments with larger patch size of plant cultivated and creating new plant patch in the vicinity, populations may achieve a reduction in travel costs and increase reliability in cultivation. This strategy may induce agglomeration of people and reduce information costs as well. As proposed by Von Thunen distance from settlement determine the type of land use within concentric zones around that settlement. Johnson explains that on the assumption that in order to minimize costs a settlement is located in the center of the resource area which its inhabitants exploit, catchment basin analysis defines the radius of that resource area as the distance beyond which energy expended equals or exceeds the energy return of exploitation. Multiple village occupation may be seen as part of the strategy to minimize costs and present the advantage of population agglomeration. Differences in village size and population

may provide information about functional size or kind of activities undertaken within the settlements and which are related to social and subsistence factors.
19. Johnson, (personal communication), does not believe so and indicates that they must just be spindle whorls.
20. Hassan indicates that perhaps Osiris may have been a king of the Delta, and his attributes may have been associated with Isis. Since this affiliation is consistent with the identification of her name with the throne: "Ist" (Hassan, 1992).
21. According to the Heliopolis' creation account, the God Atum embodied both male and female and he created the world by masturbation. Another creation account is that of the God Ptah of Memphis created the world by his word. A process of information which linked the material with the immaterial, according to Allen (1988).
22. Baines and Te Velde describe how the god Horus navigated his semen into Seth's behind and how Seth insinuated his semen into Horus' behind. Sexuality is a powerful metaphor in the relationship between Horus and Seth. These metaphors included the molestation of the child Horus by Seth, the castration of Seth by Horus and the impregnation of Seth by Horus' semen, explaining the birth of the moon (Hassan, 1992).
23. Manfred Bietak found seals impressed with motifs that resemble the Mesopotamian seal impressions on Bulae, such as rosettes (1966). This find is important because it demonstrates that the sealing system was in use from the Delta throughout Nubia since very early times.
24. This is also a depiction that has been found in the painted tomb at Hierakonpolis (Williams, 1988).

Bibliography

Adams, Barbara B. *Ancient Hierakonpolis*, 2 vols. Warminster: Aris and Phillips, 1974.

Allen, James P. "Yale Egyptological Studies." *Genesis in Egypt: The Philosophy of Ancient Egyptian Creation Accounts*, vol. 2. Ed. by William Kelly Simpson. New Haven: Yale University Press, 1988.

Amer, Moustafa "Bulletin of the Faculty of Arts, Egyptian University." *Annual Report of the Maadi Excavations, 1930-32*, vol. 1 (1933).

___ "Bulletin of the Faculty of Arts, Egyptian University." *Annual Report of the Maadi Excavations,* 1935, vol. 2 (1935).

Anderson, Wendy "Badarian Burials: Evidence of Social Inequality in Middle Egypt during the Early Predynastic Era." *Journal of the American Research in Egypt* 29 (1992).

Arkell, A.J. and Peter J. Ucko. "Review of Predynastic Development in the Nile Valley." *Current Anthropology* 6 (1965).

Arnett, William S. *The Predynastic Origin of Egyptian Hieroglyphs.* Washington, D. C.: University Press of America, 1982.

Ayrton, Edward R., C. T. Currelly and A. E. P. Weigall. "Abydos Part III." *Egyptian Exploration Society* 25. London, 1904.

Ayrton, Edward R., and W. L. S. Loat. "Predynastic Cemetery at el Mahasna." *Egyptian Exploration Society* 31. London, 1911.

Bard, Kathryn A. "An Analysis of the Predynastic Cemeteries of Naqada and Armant in Terms of Social Differentiation: The Origin of the State in Predynastic Egypt." Ph.D. diss., University of Toronto, 1987.

___ "The Geography of Excavated Predynastic Sites and the Rise of Complex Society." *Journal of American Research Center in Egypt* 24 (1987).

___ "A Quantitative Analysis of the Predynastic Burials in Armant Cemetery 1400-1500." *JEA* 74 (1988).

___ "Predynastic Settlement Patterns in the Hu-Semaineh Region, Egypt." *Journal of Field Archaeology*, vol. 16 (1989).

___ "Toward an Interpretation of the Role of Ideology in the Evolution of Complex Society in Egypt." *Journal of Anthropological Archaeology* 11 (1992).

___ "Origins of Egyptian Writing." In *The Followers of Horus: Studies Dedicated to Michael Allen Hoffman*. Ed. by Renee Friedman and Barbara Adams. Oxford: Oxbow Books, 1992.

Barich, Barbara, Fekri Hassan and Mahmoud Abdel Moneim. "L'Area Preistorica di Bahr Playa (Oasi di Farafra) e Aspetti Predinastici della Valle del Nilo." In *Sesto Congresso Internazionale di Egittologia: Atti,* vol. 1 (1992).

Baumgartel, Elise J. The Cultures of Prehistoric Egypt. Vol. 1. Published 1947, Revised edition. London: Oxford University Press, 1955.
___*The Cultures of Prehistoric Egypt.* Vol. 2. London: Oxford University Press, 1960.
___"Scorpion and Rosette and the Fragment of the Large Hierakonpolis Mace Head." In *ZAS* 93 (1966).
___"About some Ivory Statuettes from the 'Main Deposit' at Hierakonpolis." In *Jarce* 7 (1968).
___"Some Additional Remarks on the Hierakonpolis Ivories." In *Jarce* 8 (1969-1970).
___"Predynastic Egypt." *Cambridge Ancient History,* vol. 1, revised edition. London: Cabridge University Press, 1970.
___*Petrie's Naqada Excavation: A Supplement.* London: Bernard Quartich, 1970.
Beale, Thomas W. "Beveled Rim Bowls and their Implications for Change and Economic Organization in the Later Forth Millennium B.C." *Journal of Near Eastern Studies 37 No. 4, 1978.*
Bell, Barbara. "The Oldest Records of the Nile Floods." *In Geographical Journal* 73 (1970).
Bietak, Manfred. "Urban Archaeology and the 'Town Problem' in Ancient Egypt." In *Egyptology and the Social Science,* five studies, ed. by Kent R. Weeks. Cairo: The American University in Cairo Press, 1979.
Brink, van den Edwin C. M. "A Transitional Late Predynastic-Early Dynastic Settlement Site in the Northeastern Delta." In *MDAIK* 45 (1989).
___"Corpus and Numerical Evaluation of the 'Thinite' Pot Marks." *The Followers of Horus: Studies Dedicated to Michael Allen Hoffman.* Ed. by Renee Friedman and Barbara Adams. Oxford: Oxbow Books, 1992.
Brunton, Guy, E. W. Gardner and W. F. Petrie. "Qua and Badari," vol. 1. *British School of Archaeology in Egypt* 45. London: Bernard Quartich, 1927.
Brunton, Guy and Gertrude Caton-Thompson. *The Badarian Civilization and the Prehistoric Remains Near Badari.* London: Bernard Quartich, 1928.
Brunton, Guy. "The Predynastic Town-Site Hierakonpolis." *In Studies Presented to F. LL. Griffiths.* London, 1932.
___*Mostagedda and the Tasian Culture.* London: Bernard Quartich, 1937.
___*Matmar.* London: Bernard Quartich, 1948.
Butzer, Karl. "Environment and Human Ecology in Egypt during Predynastic and Early Dynastic Times." *Bull. Soc. Geo. D'Egypte* 32 (1959).
___*Early Hydraulic Civilization in Egypt: A Study in Cultural Ecology.* Chicago: The University of Chicago Press, 1976.
Caton-Thompson, Gertrude "Recent Excavations in the Fayum." *Man,* 28 (1928).
Caton-Thompson, Gertrude and E. H. Whittle. "Thermoluminescence Dating of the Badarian." *Antiquity* 49 (1975).

Collon, D. *First Impressions: Cylinder Seals in the Ancient Near East.* Chicago: The University of Chicago Press, 1987.

Debono, Fernand "Helwan-El Omari." *Fouilles du Service des Antiquities* 21 (1943).

___ "La Civilisation Predynastique d'el Omari (Nord d'Helouan). Nouvelles donnees." In *Bull. Inst. D'Eg.* 37 (1956).

Dreyer, Günter "Ein Seigel der Frühzeitlichen Königsnekropole von Abydos." In *Mitt. Dtsch Archaol. Inst. Abt. Kairo* 43 (1987).

___ "Umm el-Qaab." In *MDAIAK* 46 (1990).

___ "The Nile Delta in Transition: 4th - 3rd Millennium B.C." *Proceedings of the Seminar in Cairo, October 21-24, 1990.* Ed. and published by Edwin C. M. van den Brink, 1992.

___ "Horus Krokodil, ein Gegenkonig der Dynastie O." *In The Followers of Horus: Studies Dedicated to Michael Allen Hoffman (1944-1990).* Ed. by Renee Friedman and Barbara Adams. Oxford: Oxbow Books, 1992.

___ "Umm el-Qaab." In *MDAIAK* 49 (1993).

___ "A Hundred Years at Abydos." In *Egyptian Archaeology: The Bulletin of the Egypt Exploration Society* 3 (1993).

___ MDKI V 86 1998.

Emery, Walter B. *Excavations at Saqqara, 1937-1938: Hor-Aha.* Cairo: Government Press, 1939.

___ *Archaic Egypt.* Harmondsworth, England: Penguin Books, 1961.

___ *Great Tombs of the First Dynasty.* London: EES, 1961.

Engles, Drew R. "An Early Dynastic Cemetery at Kafr Ghattati." *Journal of American Research Center in Egypt* 27 (1990).

Fairsevis Walter A., Jr. "Preliminary Report on the First Two Seasons at Hierakonpolis." *Journal of American Research Center in Egypt* 9 (1972).

___ *Preliminary Report on Excavations at Hierakonpolis: the Season of January to March 1978 (The Work on Kom el Ahmar and Fort).* Sponsored by The American Museum of Natural History, New York, and Vassar College. Poughkeepsie, 1978.

___ "The Hierakonpolis Project No. 1: Excavation of the Temple Area on the Kom el Gemuwia Season of 1978." *Occasional Papers in Anthropology, Vassar College.* Poughkeepsie, 1983.

___ "Hierakonpolis Project No. 2: Hierakonpolis–The Graffiti and the Origins of Egyptian Hieroglphic Writing." *Occasional Papers in Anthropology, Vassar College.* Poughkeepsie, 1983.

Fischer, Henry G. "The Origin of Egyptian Hierglyphs." *In The Origins of Writing,* ed. by Wayne M. Senner. Lincoln and London: University of Nebraska Press, 1990.

Frankfort, Henri *Cylinder Seals: A Documentary Essay on the Art and Religion of the Ancient Near East.* London: MacMillan and Co., 1939.

___ *Kinship and the Gods: A Study of Ancient Near Eastern Religion as the Integration of Society and Nature.* Chicago: University of Chicago, 1948.

Gardiner, Sir Alan *Egypt of the Pharaohs.* Oxford: Oxford University Press, 1961.

___*Egyptian Grammar: Being an Introduction to the Study of Hieroglyphs,* revised third edition. Oxford: The Griffith Institute, Ashmolean Museum, 1957. Reprinted, 1982.

Geller, R. Jeremy *The Predynastic Ceramics Industry at Hierakonpolis.* Master's thesis, Washington University, St. Louis, 1984.

Gibson, M. G. "Summary." In *World Archaeology* 17 (1987).

Griswold, William A. "Measuring Social Inequality at Armant." In *The Followers of Horus,* ed. by Renee Friedman and Barbara Adams. Oxford: Oxbow Books, 1992.

Harlan, J. Fred *Predynastic Settlement Patterns: A View from Hierakonpolis.* Ph.D. diss., Washington University, St. Louis, 1985.

___"Wadi and Desert Settlement at Predynastic Hierakonpolis." In *The Followers of Horus: Studies Dedicated to Michael Allen Hoffman,* ed. by Renee Friedman and Barbara Adams. Oxford: Oxbow Books, 1992.

Hassan, Fekri Annual Meeting of American Research Center in Egypt in San Francisco, 1980. *Agricultural Developments in the Naqada Region during the Predynastic Period.*

___"The Predynastic of Egypt: Subsistence Settlements Studies: The Naqada-Hattara Region." National Science Foundation, Washington, D.C., 1981.

___"Primeval Goddess to Divine King: The Mythogenesis of Power in the Early Egyptian State." In *The Followers of Horus: Studies Dedicated to Michael Allen Hoffman,* ed. by Renee Friedman and Barbara Adms. Oxford: Oxbow Books, 1992.

Hoffman, Michael A. *Egypt Before the Pharaohs.* 2d addition. ed. London: ARK Paperbacks, 1979, edited in 1984.

___*The Predynastic of Hierakonpolis. An Interim Report.* Cairo: Egyptian Studies Association Publication No. 1 (1982).

James, T. G. H. *Excavating in Egypt: The Egypt Exploration Society 1882-1982.* 2d. ed. Ed. by T. G. H. James, London: The University of Chicago Press, 1984.

Johnson, Gregory "Local Exchange and Early Development in South Western Iran." *Anthropological Papers No. 51,* Museum of Anthropology University of Michigan, Ann Arbor, Michigan, 1973.

___"Aspects of Regional Analysis in Archaeology." *Annual Review of Anthropology* 6 (1977).

___"Spatial Organization of Early Uruk Settlement Systems," Colloques Internationaux du CNRS No. 580. *L'Archaeologie de l'Iraq: Perspectives et Limites de l'Interpretation Anthropologique des Documents.* Ed. by Marie Therese Barrelet. Paris: Centre National de la Recherche Scientifique, 1980.

___"Organizational Structure and Scalar Stress." *Theory and Explanation in Archaeology: The Southampton Conference.* Ed. by Colin Renfrew, Michael J. Rowlands and Barbara Avvott Segraves. New York: The Academic Press, 1982.

___"Late Uruk in Greater Mesopotamia: Expansion or Collapse?" *L'Interpretazione Funzionale dei Dati in Paleotologia.* Ed. by A. Palmieri. Rome: Origini-Preistoria e Protostoria della Civilta Antiche XIV, 1988-89.

___"Dynamics of Southwestern Prehistory: Far Outside Looking in." *Dynamics of Southwest Prehistory.* Ed. by Linda S. Cordell and George J. Gummerman. Washington, D.C.: Smithsonian Institute Press, 1989.

Junker, Hermann "Wien auf der Neolithischen Siedlung von Merimde-Beni Salama." *Anzeiger der Akadamie der Wissenschafften in Wien, Philosophische-Historische Klasse, 1940.*

Kaiser, Werner "Zur Inneren Chronologie der Naqadakultur." *Archaeologia Geographica* 6:69-77. Taf. 15-27, 1957.

Kantor, H. "Further Evidence for Early Mesopotamian Relations with Egypt." *Journal of Near Eastern Studies* 11 (1952).

Kaplony, Peter *Die Inschriften de Agtptischen Fruhzeit.* 3 vols. And supplement. Wiesbaden: Harrassowitz, 1963-1964.

Kees, Hermann *Ancient Egypt: A Cultural Topography.* Ed. by T. C. H. James, trans. By Ian F. D. Morrow. London: Faber and Faber, 1961.

Kemp, Barry "Abydos." In *Excavating in Egypt: The Egypt Exploration Society 1882-1982.* Ed. by T. G. H. James. 2d ed. London: The University of Chicago Press, 1984.

___*Ancient Egypt: Anatomy of a Civilization.* 2d. ed. London: Routledge, 1991.

Lucas, Alfred and J. R. Harris. *Ancient Egyptian Materials and Industries.* 4th ed. London: E. Arnold Ltd., 1962.

Menghin, Oswald "Die Grabung der Universitat Kairo bei Maadi." In *MDAIK,* 1934a.

Mond, Sir Robert and Oliver H. Myers. "Cemeteries of Armant." *Egypt Exploration Society.* London, 1937.

Mortensen, Bodil "Carbon-14 Dates from el Omari." *The Followers of Horus: Studies Dedicated to Michael Allen Hoffman.* Ed. by Renee Friedman and Barbara Adams. Oxford: Oxbow Books, 1992.

Nissen, H. J. "Aspects of Development of Early Cylinder Seals." *World Archaeology* 17 (1987).

___*The Early History of the Ancient Near East, 9000-2000 B.C.* Chicago: The University of Chicago Press, 1988.

___*Fruhe Schrift und Techniken der Wirschaftsverwaltung im Alten Vorderen Orient: Informationsspeicherung und-verarbeitung vor 5000 Jaheren.* Berlin: Verlag Franzbecker und Max-Planck-Institut fur Bildungsforschung, 1991.

Payne, Joan Crowfoot. "Predynastic Chronology at Naqada." *The Followers of Horus: Studies Dedicated to Michael Allen Hoffman.* Ed. by Renee Friedman and Barbara Adams. Oxford: Oxbow Books, 1992.

Peet, T. Eric "The Cemeteries of Abydos." *Egyptian Exploration Society.* 34 (1914).

Perez, Lagarcha "The Nile Delta during Naqada III." In *Sesto Congresso Internazionale de Egittologia: Atti.* Vol. 1 (1992).

Petrie, Sir Flienders and J. E. Quibell. *Naqada and Ballas.* London: British School of Archaeology in Egypt, 1896.

Petrie, F. *Coptos*, London: Bernard Quaritch, 1896.

___ *Diaspolis Parva: The Cemeteries of Abadiyeh and Hu.* London: Egypt Exploration Fund, 1901.

___ London: Egypt Exploration Fund, 1902.

___ *Tarkhan.* London: British School of Archaeology in Egypt, 1914.

Reisner, G. A. *The Early Dynastic Cemeteries of Nag-ed-Der.* Leipzig: J. C. Hinrichs, 1908.

Saad, Zaki *Royal Excavations at Saqqara and Helwan.* Cairo: Imprimerie de l'Institut Francais d'Archeologie Orientale, 1947.

Schmandt-Besserat, Denise. *Before Writing: From Counting to Cuneiform.* Vol. 1. Austin: University of Texas Press, 1992.

Schulman, Alan R. "Still More Egyptian Seal Impressions from 'En Besor'." *The Nile Delta in Transition; 4th-3rd Millenium B.C.* Proceedings of Seminar in Cairo, October 21-24, 1990. Ed. and published by Edwin C. M. van den Brink, 1992.

Smith, Harry S. "The Making of Egypt: A Review of the Influence of Susa and Sumer on Upper Egypt and Lower Nubia in the 4th Millennium B.C." *The Followers of Horus: Studies Dedicated to Michael Hoffman, Ed. by Renee Friedman and Barbara Adams. Oxford: Oxbow Books, 1992.*

Smith, Stevenson William *The Art and Architecture of Ancient Egypt. (The Pelican History of Art).* 2d ed. Revised by William Kelly Simpson. London: Butler & Tanner Ltd., 1981.

Trigger, Bruce G., B. J. Kemp, D. O'Connor and A. B. Lloyd. *Ancient Egypt: A Social History.* Cambridge: Cambridge University Press, 1983.

Trigger, Bruce G. *Early Civilizations: Ancient Egypt in Context.* Cairo: The American University in Cairo Press, 1993.

Vermeersch, Pierre "Les Fouilles d'El Kab." *Zeitschrift fur Agyptische Sprache und Altertumskunde* 17 (1969).

Way, Thomas von der V. "Tell el Fara'in-Buto." In *MDAIK* 43 (1983).

___ "Indications of Architecture with Niches at Buto." *The Followers of Horus: Studies Dedicated to Michael Allen Hoffman,* ed. by Renee Friedman and Barbara Adams. Oxford: Oxbow Books, 1992.

Wenke, Robert J. "Egypt: Origin of Complex Societies." In *Annual Review of Anthropolgy* 18 (1989).

___"The Neolithic-Predynastic Transition in the Fayum Depression." In *The Followers of Horus: Studies Dedicated to Michael Allen Hoffman*, ed. by Renee Friedman and Barbara Adams. Oxford: Oxbow Books, 1992.

Williams, Bruce B. "The Lost Pharaohs of Nubia." In *Archaeology* 33, no. 5 (September-October 1980).

___"The A-Group Royal Cemetery at Qustul: Cemetery 'L'," Part I. In *The University of Chicago between Abu Simbel and the Sudan*, vol. 3. Chicago, 1986.

___"Narmer and the Coptos Colossi." In *JARCE*, vol. 25 (1988).

Wilson, John "Buto and Hierakonpolis." In *JARCE* 14 (1955).